Conference on Empirical Methods in Natural Language Processing (EMNLP 2022)

Tutorial Abstracts

Abu Dhabi, United Arab Emirates and Online
7-11 December 2022

ISBN: 978-1-7138-9095-9

Printed from e-media with permission by:

Curran Associates, Inc.
57 Morehouse Lane
Red Hook, NY 12571

CURRAN ASSOCIATES INC.
proceedings
.com

Some format issues inherent in the e-media version may also appear in this print version.

Printed with permission by Curran Associates, Inc. (2024)

For permission requests, please contact the Association for Computational Linguistics at the address below.

Association for Computational Linguistics
209 N. Eighth Street
Stroudsburg, Pennsylvania 18360

Phone: 1-570-476-8006
Fax: 1-570-476-0860

acl@aclweb.org

Additional copies of this publication are available from:

Curran Associates, Inc.
57 Morehouse Lane
Red Hook, NY 12571 USA
Phone: 845-758-0400
Fax: 845-758-2633
Email: curran@proceedings.com
Web: www.proceedings.com

EMNLP 2022

The 2022 Conference on Empirical Methods in Natural Language Processing: Tutorial Abstracts

Tutorial Abstracts

December 7-8, 2022

Introduction

Welcome to the Tutorials Session of EMNLP 2022

The EMNLP 2022 tutorials session provides an in depth coverage of a variety of topics reflecting recent advances in Natural Language Processing methods and applications, presented by experts from academia and ranging from introductory to cutting-edge.

This year, as has been the tradition over the past few years, the call, submission, reviewing and selection of tutorials were coordinated jointly for multiple conferences: ACL, NAACL, COLING and EMNLP. A review committee consisting of ACL, NAACL, COLING and EMNLP tutorial chairs as well as 23 external reviewers (see Program Committee for the full list), was formed. The committee followed a review process that ensured that each of the 47 submitted tutorial proposals, received 3 reviews. The selection criteria included clarity and preparedness, novelty or timely character of the topic, instructors' experience, likely audience interest, open access of the tutorial instructional material, and diversity and inclusion.
The six tutorials selected for EMNLP include 2 introductory tutorials and 4 cutting-edge tutorials. The two introductory tutorials address Arabic natural language processing (T2) and causal inference for natural language processing(T4) while the cutting-edge tutorials address meaning representations for natural languages (T1), emergent language-based coordination in deep Multi-Agent Systems (T3), modular and parameter-efficient fine-tuning for NLP models (T5), and non-autoregressive models for fast sequence generation (T6).

We would like to thank the ACL, NAACL, and COLING tutorial chairs and the 23 external reviewers for their effective collaboration and their efforts to ensure a smooth selection process as well as their invaluable assistance in the decision process. We would also like to thank EMNLP's general chair Noah Smith for his readiness to extend support whenever requested. We are very grateful for tutorial organizers for their valuable contributions.

As has been the case last year, tutorial presentations will be a mixture of online, on-site and hybrid presentations. We hope you all benefit from and enjoy the tutorial program at EMNLP 2022!

EMNLP 2022 Tutorial Co-chairs
Samhaa R. El-Beltagy
Xipeng Qiu

Organizing Committee

General Chair

Noah Smith, University of Washington/Allen Institute for Artificial Intelligence

Program Chairs

Yoav Goldberg, Bar Ilan University, Isreal
Zornitsa Kozareva, SliceX AI, USA
Yue Zhang, Westlake University, China

Tutorial Chairs

Samhaa R. El-Beltagy, Newgiza University, Egypt
Xipeng Qiu, Fudan University, China

Program Committee

Program Committee

Cecilia Alm, Rochester Institute of Technology, USA
Antonios Anastasopoulos, George Mason University, USA
Miguel Ballesteros, Amazon, USA
Daniel Beck, University of Melbourne, Australia
Luciana Benotti, National University of Córdoba, Argentina
Yevgeni Berzak, Technion, Israel Institute of Technology, Israel
Erik Cambria, Nanyang Technological University, Singapore
Hsin-Hsi Chen, National Taiwan University, Taiwan
Gaël Dias, University of Caen Normandy, France
Lucia Donatelli, Saarland University, Germany
Samhaa R. El-Beltagy, Newgiza University, Egypt
Karën Fort, Sorbonne Université / LORIA, France
Heng Ji, University of Illinois, Urbana-Champaign, USA
David Jurgens, University of Michigan, USA
Naoaki Okazaki, Tokyo Institute of Technology, Japan
Alexis Palmer, University of Colorado, Boulder, USA
Mohammad Taher Pilehvar, Tehran Institute for Advanced Studies, Iran
Barbara Plank, LMU Munich, Germany and IT University of Copenhagen, Denmark
Emily Prud'hommeaux, Boston College, USA
Xipeng Qiu, Fudan University, China
Agata Savary, Université Paris-Saclay, France
João Sedoc, New York University, USA
Yulia Tsvetkov, University of Washington, USA
Aline Villavicencio, University of Sheffield, UK
Ivan Vulić, University of Cambridge, UK
Yogarshi Vyas, Amazon, USA
Joachim Wagner, Dublin City University, Ireland
Taro Watanabe, Nara Institute of Science and Technology, Japan
Aaron Steven White, University of Rochester, USA
Diyi Yang, Georgia Institute of Technology, USA
Marcos Zampieri, Rochester Institute of Technology, USA
Meishan Zhang, Harbin Institute of Technology (Shenzhen), China
Yue Zhang, Westlake University, China
Arkaitz Zubiaga, Queen Mary University London, UK

Table of Contents

Program

Wednesday, December 7, 2022

09:00 - 17:30 *Day 1*

Meaning Representations for Natural Languages: Design, Models and Applications
Jeffrey Flanigan, Ishan Jindal, Yunyao Li, Tim O'Gorman, Martha Palmer and Nianwen Xue

Arabic Natural Language Processing
Nizar Habash

Emergent Language-Based Coordination In Deep Multi-Agent Systems
Marco Baroni, Roberto Dessi and Angeliki Lazaridou

Thursday, December 8, 2022

09:00 - 17:30 *Day 2*

CausalNLP Tutorial: An Introduction to Causality for Natural Language Processing
Zhijing Jin, Amir Feder and Kun Zhang

Modular and Parameter-Efficient Fine-Tuning for NLP Models
Sebastian Ruder, Jonas Pfeiffer and Ivan Vulić

Meaning Representations for Natural Languages: Design, Models and Applications
Jeffrey Flanigan, Ishan Jindal, Yunyao Li, Tim O'Gorman, Martha Palmer and Nianwen Xue

Meaning Representations for Natural Languages: Design, Models and Applications

[†]Jeffrey Flanigan, [◇]Tim O'Gorman, [‡]Ishan Jindal, [‡]Yunyao Li, Martha Palmer, [◇]Nianwen Xue
[†]jmflanig@ucsc.edu, [◇]timjogorman@gmail.com, [‡]ishan.jindal@ibm.com,
[‡]yunyaoli@us.ibm.com, palmer@colorado.edu, [◇]xuen@brandeis.edu

Abstract

This tutorial reviews the design of common meaning representations, SoTA models for predicting meaning representations, and the applications of meaning representations in a wide range of downstream NLP tasks and real-world applications. Reporting by a diverse team of NLP researchers from academia and industry with extensive experience in designing, building and using meaning representations, our tutorial has three components: (1) an introduction to common meaning representations, including basic concepts and design challenges; (2) a review of SoTA methods on building models for meaning representations; and (3) an overview of applications of meaning representations in downstream NLP tasks and real-world applications. We will also present qualitative comparisons of common meaning representations and a quantitative study on how their differences impact model performance. Finally, we will share best practices in choosing the right meaning representation for downstream tasks.

1 Background

In this tutorial, we primarily discuss one thread of meaning representations encompassing the Proposition Bank (PropBank) (Palmer et al., 2005), Abstract Meaning Representations (AMR) as well as Uniform Meaning Representations (UMR), a recent extension to AMR. We will discuss the representations themselves, discuss the latest semantic role labeling (SRL) and AMR parsing techniques using these representations, and overview applications of these meaning representations to practical natural language applications.

These approaches all share the use of the predicate-specific semantic roles defined in the Proposition Bank (PropBank) (Palmer et al., 2005). In such an approach, the particular sense of "afford" in "The public was afforded a preview of the show", is sense-tagged as "afford.02" in PropBank, and it requires three semantic roles, *Arg0* the provider, *Arg1* the thing that is provided, and *Arg2* the recipient of *Arg1*. We will seek to provide attendees with good intuitions about the behavior and advantages of how such predicate-specific roles work across these different meaning representations. We will also contextualize how such an approach to semantics compares to other approaches such as FrameNet(Baker et al., 1998).

AMR can be viewed as an extension of PropBank to handle wide-coverage sentence representation. Whereas PropBank is annotated on a predicate-by-predicate basis and predicates are can be viewed as independent, Abstract Meaning Representation (AMR) (Banarescu et al., 2013) adopts PropBank-style semantic roles but also connects the different predicates in a sentence in a graph. Such an AMR graph seeks to represent the meaning of sentences as a single-rooted directed acyclic graph, where the nodes are labeled with entity or predicate types, and edges are labeled with semantic roles (e.g., Arg0, Arg1) or general semantic relations (e.g., *time*, *location*).

AMR captures the essential predicate-argument structure of a sentence that is applicable to a variety of applications as well as to languages such as Chinese. Extensions to AMR attempt to increase coverage beyond the sentence, to add additional semantic phenomena, and to increase cross-linguistic applicability(Gysel et al., 2021). We discuss these extensions with a focus on the new Uniform Meaning Representation(UMR) approach, which extends AMR to add coverage of *Aspect*, *Scope*, *Person* and *Number* annotation to the sentence level representation, adds a document-level representation that captures temporal and modal dependencies as well as coreference relations that can go beyond sentence boundaries, and which defines conventions for AMR-style annotation of languages without existing PropBank lexicons. The discussion of UMR will provide attendees with an understanding of

Proceedings of the 2022 Conference on Empirical Methods in Natural Language Processing: Tutorial Abstracts, pages 1 - 8
December 7-8, 2022

which semantic phenomena are out of scope for AMR and how projects like UMR address them.

In this tutorial we will provide an in-depth discussion of these meaning representations. When doing so, we will also discuss how they are similar to or different from other meaning representations such as semantic dependencies (Oepen et al., 2015), Minimal Recursion Semantics (MRS) (Copestake et al., 2005), Discourse Representation Theory (DRT) (Kamp and Reyle, 2013; Bos et al., 2017) , and UCCA (Abend and Rappoport, 2013).

The increasing availability of meaning representation datasets such as PropBank as well as significant advances in modeling techniques have led to increased interest and progress in computational models for meaning representation parsers. In this tutorial, we will discuss models for SRL and AMR tasks. We will start with the traditional SRL models that rely heavily on syntactic feature templates (Xue and Palmer, 2004; Pradhan et al., 2005; Zhao et al., 2009; Akbik and Li, 2016), go on to advanced neural SRL models (He et al., 2017, 2018), and include more recent work (Marcheggiani and Titov, 2020; Fei et al., 2021a,b). For AMR parsing, we will cover early approaches and SoTA methods for graph-based methods (Flanigan et al., 2014; Foland and Martin, 2017; Lyu and Titov, 2018; Cai and Lam, 2019; Zhang et al., 2019b; Zhou et al., 2020), transition-based methods (Wang et al., 2015; Wang and Xue, 2017; Ballesteros and Al-Onaizan, 2017; Fernandez Astudillo et al., 2020; Zhou et al., 2021), grammar-based methods(Peng et al., 2015; Artzi et al., 2015; Chen et al., 2018) sequence-to-sequence methods(Konstas et al., 2017; Xu et al., 2020), and other methods (Pust et al., 2015; Welch et al., 2018; Lindemann et al., 2020; Cai and Lam, 2020; Lee et al., 2020; Lam et al., 2021). We will discuss whole-document AMR parsing (Anikina et al., 2020; Fu et al., 2021).

There is a wide range of NLP tasks that leverage meaning representations as an effective way to infuse knowledge into their models for better performance and interpretability. For instance, SRL has been widely used to build better models for information extraction, such as open information extraction (Christensen et al., 2010; Solawetz and Larson, 2021) and event extraction (Zhang et al., 2020a, 2021), opinion mining (Marasović and Frank, 2018; Zhang et al., 2019a), machine translation (Bastings et al., 2017), natural language inference (Zhang et al., 2020b), and reading comprehension (Guo et al., 2020). Similarly, AMR has been adopted for a variety of downstream NLP tasks such as information extraction (Pan et al., 2015; Garg et al., 2016; Rao et al., 2017), summarization (Liu et al., 2015; Liao et al., 2018), machine translation (Song et al., 2019; Nguyen et al., 2021), question answering (Sachan and Xing, 2016; Mitra and Baral, 2016; Kapanipathi et al., 2021), and dialog (Bonial et al., 2020; Bai et al., 2021). With the increasing availability of high-quality meaning representation parsers, we also see increasing adoption of meaning representation in wide-range of real-world applications, from an enterprise-grade contract understanding system (Agarwal et al., 2021) to customizable targeted sentiment analysis.

2 Tutorial type

We are proposing a 6-hour cutting edge tutorial to cover in depth on the design, modeling, and application of meaning representations.

3 Outline of the tutorial

The proposed tutorial is organized as follows:
I. Introduction (15 minutes). We will provide a high-level overview and evolution of common meaning representation, discussing key concepts, unique challenges and examples of applications.
II. Common Meaning Representations (150 minutes) In this section, we will provide an in-depth review of three common meaning representation – PropBank and FrameNet that have been widely used to train Semantic Role Labeling systems, Abstract Meaning Representation, a sentence-level meaning representation that inherits PropBank-style semantic roles, and Uniform Meaning Representation, a cross-lingual document-level meaning representation that to a large extent inherits the sentence-level representation of AMR. We also provide a brief overview of other common meaning representations as a brief background. We will also discuss the unique challenges around designing meaning representation. Concretely, we will organize this section as follows:

- **PropBank** We start out our discussion with PropBank-style semantic roles and their theoretical underpinnings. In particular, we will discuss the proto-roles of Dowty (Dowty, 1991). We will go over the process of developing the frame files, and how the frame files are used to annotate each predicate instances in the corpus. We will discuss how to annotate complicated predicates such as phrasal verbs and light verb constructions, and end with a brief discussion of how PropBank-style semantic roles are related to FrameNet (Baker et al., 1998) and VerbNet (Schuler, 2005).

- **Abstract Meaning Representation (AMR)** We next discuss different aspects of AMR, and cover how AMR represents word senses, semantic roles, named entity types, date entity types, and relations.
- **Uniform Meaning Representation (UMR)** Finally we will discuss Uniform Meaning Representations, and discuss how UMR builds on AMR. We will also discuss the cross-lingual aspect of UMR.
- **Other Related Meaning Representations** We will provide a brief overview on other common meaning representations such as MRS, etc.
- **Comparison of Meaning Representations** We will then present a qualitative comparison of the three meaning representations on their commonalities and differences.
- **Building Meaning Representation Datasets** Finally, we will close this section with discussions on the general approaches, challenges, and emerging trend in building datasets for meaning representations.

III. Modeling Meaning Representation (100 minutes) We will next discuss computational models for SRL and AMR parsing, from early approaches to current end-to-end SoTA methods. We will discuss gaps and challenges in building and evaluating such models. We will also share a quantitative comparison study based on SoTA models and demonstrates how the differences of the meaning representations lead to differences in model performance on various examples.

IV. Applying Meaning Representation (75 minutes) We will share applications of the meaning representations for a wide range of tasks from information extraction to question answering. We will discuss how the differences in these meaning representations discussed earlier impact the choice of which one(s) to use for which downstream tasks.

V. Open Questions and Future work (15 minutes) We will conclude the tutorial by raising several open research questions in this space (e.g., creating datasets for training and evaluation at scale) and ways we as a community might work forward on these issues.

4 Breadth of the tutorial

This tutorial will have three components. The first component (45%) will introduce core concepts related to meaning representations, common meaning representations and key challenges in designing (including scaling to different languages) and developing those meaning representations. The second component (30%) will review the state-of-the-art models for two common meaning representations: SRL and AMR. It will also provide a quantitative comparison study of how the differences in meaning representations impact model performance. Finally, the last component (25%) will show how real-world applications as well as research projects leverage meaning representations for better performance and more transparency and how to decide which meaning representation to use based on downstream tasks.

5 Diversity of the team

This tutorial is to be given a team of researchers from five different institutions across academia and industry, both junior instructors (including 1 assistant professor, and 2 junior industry researcher) and researchers with extensive experience in academic and corporate research settings. The team includes creators, modelers, and users of common meaning representations. The team also has a good gender balance (two female and four male instructors).

6 Target audience and objectives

This tutorial welcomes all stakeholders in the NLP community, including NLP researchers, domain-specific practitioners, and students. In this tutorial, attendees will

- Develop fluency in core concepts of common meaning representations, state-of-the-art models for producing these meaning representations, and potential use cases.
- Gain insights into the practical benefits and challenges around leveraging meaning representations for downstream applications.
- Discuss and reflect on open questions related to meaning representations.

7 Prerequisites

As stated before, our tutorial presumes no prior knowledge on the core concepts of meaning representation. However, a basic understanding of NLP, machine learning (especially, deep learning) concepts may be helpful. We intend to introduce the necessary concepts related to meaning representation during the introductory section of the tutorial.

8 Reading list

We aim to make the tutorial self-contained, but it will be helpful if the attendees can get some basic understanding of this field by going through the following reading list: PropBank: (Palmer et al., 2005), AMR: (Banarescu et al., 2013), UMR: (Gysel et al., 2021), SRL models: (Pradhan et al., 2005; He et al., 2017), and AMR models: (Flanigan et al., 2014; Lyu and Titov, 2018; Xu et al., 2020).

9 Audience size estimation

We are proposing a cutting edge tutorial on meaning representation. No similar tutorial has been given in ACL/EMNLP/NAACL/COLING in the past five years. Since meaning representation is an important topic in NLP, we expect that this tutorial will be popular with 50 - 100 attendees.

10 Open Access

We agree to allow the publication of our slides and video recording of our tutorial in the ACL Anthology.

11 Technique Equipment

To give this tutorial, we need to have internet access and a projector or large screen. No special requirements needed.

12 Preferred Venue

Due to travel restrictions of our instructors, we prefer NAACL and ACL over the other venues.

13 Ethics Statement

Infusing meaning representations into NLP models are shown to be effective in injecting knowledge into such models. As such, meaning representations allow deep understanding of languages and identify more nuanced instances of ethics concerns (e.g. biases). Furthermore, meaning representations allow the building of fully interpretable yet effective models. We hope that this tutorial helps the audience to develop a deeper appreciation for such topics and equips them with powerful tools to mitigate recent concerns that have arisen with NLP models with regard to explainability and bias.

14 Author biographies

Martha Palmer is the Helen & Hubert Croft Professor of Engineering in the Computer Science Department, and Arts & Sciences Professor of Distinction for Linguistics, at the University of Colorado, with over 300 peer-reviewed publications. Her research is focused on capturing elements of the meanings of words that can comprise automatic representations of complex sentences and documents in many languages. She is a co-Director of CLEAR, an ACL Fellow, and an AAAI Fellow.

Nianwen Xue is a Professor in the Computer Science Department and the Language & Linguistics Program at Brandeis University. His core research interests include developing linguistic corpora annotated with syntactic, semantic, and discourse structures, as well as machine learning approaches to syntactic, semantic and discourse parsing. He is an action editor for Computational Linguistics.

Ishan Jindal is a Research Staff Member with IBM Research - Almaden. His research interest lies at the intersection of machine learning and NLP, primarily in semantic parsing and model analysis for enterprise use cases. He regularly publishes papers at ML and NLP conferences.

Jeffrey Flanigan is an Assistant Professor in the Computer Science and Engineering Department at University of California Santa Cruz. He research interests are in semantic parsing and generation, with a focus on AMR, and using semantic representations in downstream applications such as summarization and machine translation. Previously he has given a tutorial in AMR at NAACL 2015.

Tim O'Gorman is a Senior Research Scientist at Thorn. He was involved in AMR 2.0 and 3.0 annotations, the Multi-sentence AMR corpus, and updates to PropBank. He co-organized the CoNLL'19 and '20 Meaning Representation Parsing shared task. His interests are in the extensions of meaning representations to cross-sentence phenomena.

Yunyao Li is a Distinguished Research Staff Member and Senior Research Manager with IBM Research - Almaden. Her expertise is at the intersection of NLP, databases, HCI, and information retrieval. Her work has resulted in 80+ peer-reviewed publications and transferred into 20+ commercial products. She regularly gives talks and tutorials, such as Explainability for NLP (AACL'20, KDD'21), and Deep Learning on Graphs for NLP (NAACL'21, KDD'21, IJCAI'21). She is an ACM Distinguished Member.

References

Omri Abend and Ari Rappoport. 2013. Universal conceptual cognitive annotation (ucca). In *Proceedings of the 51st Annual Meeting of the Association for Computational Linguistics (Volume 1: Long Papers)*, pages 228–238.

Arvind Agarwal, Laura Chiticariu, Poornima Chozhiyath Raman, Marina Danilevsky, Diman Ghazi, Ankush Gupta, Shanmukha C. Guttula, Yannis Katsis, Rajasekar Krishnamurthy, Yunyao Li, Shubham Mudgal, Vitobha Munigala, Nicholas Phan, Dhaval Sonawane, Sneha Srinivasan, Sudarshan R. Thitte, Mitesh Vasa, Ramiya Venkatachalam, Vinitha Yaski, and Huaiyu Zhu. 2021. Development of an enterprise-grade contract understanding system. In *Proceedings of the 2021 Conference of the North American Chapter of the Association for Computational Linguistics: Human Language Technologies: Industry Papers, NAACL-HLT 2021, Online, June 6-11, 2021*, pages 222–229. Association for Computational Linguistics.

Alan Akbik and Yunyao Li. 2016. K-SRL: Instance-based learning for semantic role labeling. In *Proceedings of COLING 2016, the 26th International Conference on Computational Linguistics: Technical Papers*, pages 599–608, Osaka, Japan. The COLING 2016 Organizing Committee.

Tatiana Anikina, Alexander Koller, and Michael Roth. 2020. Predicting coreference in Abstract Meaning Representations. In *Proceedings of the Third Workshop on Computational Models of Reference, Anaphora and Coreference*, pages 33–38, Barcelona, Spain (online). Association for Computational Linguistics.

Yoav Artzi, Kenton Lee, and Luke Zettlemoyer. 2015. Broad-coverage CCG semantic parsing with AMR. In *Proceedings of the 2015 Conference on Empirical Methods in Natural Language Processing*, pages 1699–1710, Lisbon, Portugal. Association for Computational Linguistics.

Xuefeng Bai, Yulong Chen, Linfeng Song, and Yue Zhang. 2021. Semantic representation for dialogue modeling. In *Proceedings of the 59th Annual Meeting of the Association for Computational Linguistics and the 11th International Joint Conference on Natural Language Processing (Volume 1: Long Papers)*, pages 4430–4445, Online. Association for Computational Linguistics.

Collin F Baker, Charles J Fillmore, and John B Lowe. 1998. The berkeley framenet project. In *36th Annual Meeting of the Association for Computational Linguistics and 17th International Conference on Computational Linguistics, Volume 1*, pages 86–90.

Miguel Ballesteros and Yaser Al-Onaizan. 2017. AMR parsing using stack-LSTMs. In *Proceedings of the 2017 Conference on Empirical Methods in Natural Language Processing*, pages 1269–1275, Copenhagen, Denmark. Association for Computational Linguistics.

Laura Banarescu, Claire Bonial, Shu Cai, Madalina Georgescu, Kira Griffitt, Ulf Hermjakob, Kevin Knight, Philipp Koehn, Martha Palmer, and Nathan Schneider. 2013. Abstract Meaning Representation for sembanking. In *Proceedings of the 7th Linguistic Annotation Workshop and Interoperability with Discourse*, pages 178–186, Sofia, Bulgaria. Association for Computational Linguistics.

Jasmijn Bastings, Ivan Titov, W. Aziz, Diego Marcheggiani, and Khalil Sima'an. 2017. Graph convolutional encoders for syntax-aware neural machine translation. In *EMNLP*.

Claire Bonial, Lucia Donatelli, Mitchell Abrams, Stephanie M. Lukin, Stephen Tratz, Matthew Marge, Ron Artstein, David Traum, and Clare Voss. 2020. Dialogue-AMR: Abstract Meaning Representation for dialogue. In *Proceedings of the Twelfth Language Resources and Evaluation Conference*, pages 684–695, Marseille, France. European Language Resources Association.

Johan Bos, Valerio Basile, Kilian Evang, Noortje Venhuizen, and Johannes Bjerva. 2017. The groningen meaning bank. In Nancy Ide and James Pustejovsky, editors, *Handbook of Linguistic Annotation*, volume 2, pages 463–496. Springer.

Deng Cai and Wai Lam. 2019. Core semantic first: A top-down approach for amr parsing. *arXiv preprint arXiv:1909.04303*.

Deng Cai and Wai Lam. 2020. Amr parsing via graph-sequence iterative inference. *arXiv preprint arXiv:2004.05572*.

Yufei Chen, Weiwei Sun, and Xiaojun Wan. 2018. Accurate SHRG-based semantic parsing. In *Proceedings of the 56th Annual Meeting of the Association for Computational Linguistics (Volume 1: Long Papers)*, pages 408–418, Melbourne, Australia. Association for Computational Linguistics.

Janara Christensen, Mausam, Stephen Soderland, and Oren Etzioni. 2010. Semantic role labeling for open information extraction. In *Proceedings of the NAACL HLT 2010 First International Workshop on Formalisms and Methodology for Learning by Reading*, pages 52–60, Los Angeles, California. Association for Computational Linguistics.

Ann Copestake, Dan Flickinger, Carl Pollard, and Ivan A Sag. 2005. Minimal recursion semantics: An introduction. *Research on language and computation*, 3(2):281–332.

David Dowty. 1991. Thematic proto-roles and argument selection. *language*, 67(3):547–619.

Hao Fei, Fei Li, Bobo Li, and Donghong Ji. 2021a. Encoder-decoder based unified semantic role labeling with label-aware syntax. In *Proc. AAAI Conf. Artif. Intell.*, pages 1479–1488.

Hao Fei, Meishan Zhang, Bobo Li, and Donghong Ji. 2021b. End-to-end semantic role labeling with neural transition-based model. In *Proc. AAAI Conf. Artif. Intell.*, pages 566–575.

Ramón Fernandez Astudillo, Miguel Ballesteros, Tahira Naseem, Austin Blodgett, and Radu Florian. 2020. Transition-based parsing with stack-transformers. In *Findings of the Association for Computational Linguistics: EMNLP 2020*, pages 1001–1007, Online. Association for Computational Linguistics.

Jeffrey Flanigan, Sam Thomson, Jaime Carbonell, Chris Dyer, and Noah A. Smith. 2014. A discriminative graph-based parser for the Abstract Meaning Representation. In *Proceedings of the 52nd Annual Meeting of the Association for Computational Linguistics (Volume 1: Long Papers)*, pages 1426–1436, Baltimore, Maryland. Association for Computational Linguistics.

William Foland and James H. Martin. 2017. Abstract Meaning Representation parsing using LSTM recurrent neural networks. In *Proceedings of the 55th Annual Meeting of the Association for Computational Linguistics (Volume 1: Long Papers)*, pages 463–472, Vancouver, Canada. Association for Computational Linguistics.

Qiankun Fu, Linfeng Song, Wenyu Du, and Yue Zhang. 2021. End-to-end AMR coreference resolution. In *Proceedings of the 59th Annual Meeting of the Association for Computational Linguistics and the 11th International Joint Conference on Natural Language Processing (Volume 1: Long Papers)*, pages 4204–4214, Online. Association for Computational Linguistics.

Sahil Garg, Aram Galstyan, Ulf Hermjakob, and Daniel Marcu. 2016. Extracting biomolecular interactions using semantic parsing of biomedical text. In *Thirtieth AAAI Conference on Artificial Intelligence*.

Shaoru Guo, Yong Guan, Ru Li, Xiaoli Li, and Hongye Tan. 2020. Incorporating syntax and frame semantics in neural network for machine reading comprehension. In *COLING*.

Jens E. L. Van Gysel, Meagan Vigus, Jayeol Chun, Kenneth Lai, Sarah Moeller, Jiarui Yao, Timothy J. O'Gorman, Andrew Cowell, W. Bruce Croft, Chu Ren Huang, Jan Hajic, James H. Martin, Stephan Oepen, Martha Palmer, James Pustejovsky, Rosa Vallejos, and Nianwen Xue. 2021. Designing a uniform meaning representation for natural language processing. *Künstliche Intelligenz*, pages 1–18.

Luheng He, Kenton Lee, Mike Lewis, and Luke Zettlemoyer. 2017. Deep semantic role labeling: What works and what's next. In *Proceedings of the 55th Annual Meeting of the Association for Computational Linguistics (Volume 1: Long Papers)*, pages 473–483, Vancouver, Canada. Association for Computational Linguistics.

Shexia He, Zuchao Li, Hai Zhao, and Hongxiao Bai. 2018. Syntax for semantic role labeling, to be, or not to be. In *Proceedings of the 56th Annual Meeting of the Association for Computational Linguistics (Volume 1: Long Papers)*, pages 2061–2071, Melbourne, Australia. Association for Computational Linguistics.

Hans Kamp and Uwe Reyle. 2013. *From discourse to logic: Introduction to modeltheoretic semantics of natural language, formal logic and discourse representation theory*, volume 42. Springer Science & Business Media.

Pavan Kapanipathi, Ibrahim Abdelaziz, Srinivas Ravishankar, Salim Roukos, Alexander Gray, Ramón Fernandez Astudillo, Maria Chang, Cristina Cornelio, Saswati Dana, Achille Fokoue, Dinesh Garg, Alfio Gliozzo, Sairam Gurajada, Hima Karanam, Naweed Khan, Dinesh Khandelwal, Young-Suk Lee, Yunyao Li, Francois Luus, Ndivhuwo Makondo, Nandana Mihindukulasooriya, Tahira Naseem, Sumit Neelam, Lucian Popa, Revanth Gangi Reddy, Ryan Riegel, Gaetano Rossiello, Udit Sharma, G P Shrivatsa Bhargav, and Mo Yu. 2021. Leveraging Abstract Meaning Representation for knowledge base question answering. In *Findings of the Association for Computational Linguistics: ACL-IJCNLP 2021*, pages 3884–3894, Online. Association for Computational Linguistics.

Ioannis Konstas, Srinivasan Iyer, Mark Yatskar, Yejin Choi, and Luke Zettlemoyer. 2017. Neural AMR: Sequence-to-sequence models for parsing and generation. In *Proceedings of the 55th Annual Meeting of the Association for Computational Linguistics (Volume 1: Long Papers)*, pages 146–157, Vancouver, Canada. Association for Computational Linguistics.

Hoang Thanh Lam, Gabriele Picco, Yufang Hou, Young-Suk Lee, Lam M. Nguyen, Dzung T. Phan, Vanessa López, and Ramón Fernandez Astudillo. 2021. Ensembling graph predictions for AMR parsing. *CoRR*, abs/2110.09131.

Young-Suk Lee, Ramon Fernandez Astudillo, Tahira Naseem, Revanth Gangi Reddy, Radu Florian, and Salim Roukos. 2020. Pushing the limits of amr parsing with self-learning. *arXiv preprint arXiv:2010.10673*.

Kexin Liao, Logan Lebanoff, and Fei Liu. 2018. Abstract meaning representation for multi-document summarization. *arXiv preprint arXiv:1806.05655*.

Matthias Lindemann, Jonas Groschwitz, and Alexander Koller. 2020. Fast semantic parsing with welltypedness guarantees. In *Proceedings of the 2020*

Conference on Empirical Methods in Natural Language Processing (EMNLP), pages 3929–3951, Online. Association for Computational Linguistics.

Fei Liu, Jeffrey Flanigan, Sam Thomson, Norman Sadeh, and Noah A. Smith. 2015. Toward abstractive summarization using semantic representations. In *Proceedings of the 2015 Conference of the North American Chapter of the Association for Computational Linguistics: Human Language Technologies*, pages 1077–1086, Denver, Colorado. Association for Computational Linguistics.

Chunchuan Lyu and Ivan Titov. 2018. AMR parsing as graph prediction with latent alignment. In *Proceedings of the 56th Annual Meeting of the Association for Computational Linguistics (Volume 1: Long Papers)*, pages 397–407, Melbourne, Australia. Association for Computational Linguistics.

Ana Marasović and Anette Frank. 2018. Srl4orl: Improving opinion role labeling using multi-task learning with semantic role labeling. In *NAACL*.

Diego Marcheggiani and Ivan Titov. 2020. Graph convolutions over constituent trees for syntax-aware semantic role labeling. In *Proceedings of the 2020 Conference on Empirical Methods in Natural Language Processing (EMNLP)*, pages 3915–3928, Online. Association for Computational Linguistics.

Arindam Mitra and Chitta Baral. 2016. Addressing a question answering challenge by combining statistical methods with inductive rule learning and reasoning. In *Proceedings of the AAAI Conference on Artificial Intelligence*, volume 30.

Long HB Nguyen, Viet H Pham, and Dien Dinh. 2021. Improving neural machine translation with amr semantic graphs. *Mathematical Problems in Engineering*, 2021.

Stephan Oepen, Marco Kuhlmann, Yusuke Miyao, Daniel Zeman, Silvie Cinková, Dan Flickinger, Jan Hajic, and Zdenka Uresova. 2015. Semeval 2015 task 18: Broad-coverage semantic dependency parsing. In *Proceedings of the 9th International Workshop on Semantic Evaluation (SemEval 2015)*, pages 915–926.

Martha Palmer, Daniel Gildea, and Paul Kingsbury. 2005. The proposition bank: An annotated corpus of semantic roles. *Computational linguistics*, 31(1):71–106.

Xiaoman Pan, Taylor Cassidy, Ulf Hermjakob, Heng Ji, and Kevin Knight. 2015. Unsupervised entity linking with Abstract Meaning Representation. In *Proceedings of the 2015 Conference of the North American Chapter of the Association for Computational Linguistics: Human Language Technologies*, pages 1130–1139, Denver, Colorado. Association for Computational Linguistics.

Xiaochang Peng, Linfeng Song, and Daniel Gildea. 2015. A synchronous hyperedge replacement grammar based approach for AMR parsing. In *Proceedings of the Nineteenth Conference on Computational Natural Language Learning*, pages 32–41, Beijing, China. Association for Computational Linguistics.

Sameer Pradhan, Wayne Ward, Kadri Hacioglu, James Martin, and Daniel Jurafsky. 2005. Semantic role labeling using different syntactic views. In *Proceedings of the 43rd Annual Meeting of the Association for Computational Linguistics (ACL'05)*, pages 581–588, Ann Arbor, Michigan. Association for Computational Linguistics.

Michael Pust, Ulf Hermjakob, Kevin Knight, Daniel Marcu, and Jonathan May. 2015. Parsing English into Abstract Meaning Representation using syntax-based machine translation. In *Proceedings of the 2015 Conference on Empirical Methods in Natural Language Processing*, pages 1143–1154, Lisbon, Portugal. Association for Computational Linguistics.

Sudha Rao, Daniel Marcu, Kevin Knight, and Hal Daumé III. 2017. Biomedical event extraction using Abstract Meaning Representation. In *BioNLP 2017*, pages 126–135, Vancouver, Canada,. Association for Computational Linguistics.

Mrinmaya Sachan and Eric Xing. 2016. Machine comprehension using rich semantic representations. In *Proceedings of the 54th Annual Meeting of the Association for Computational Linguistics (Volume 2: Short Papers)*, pages 486–492, Berlin, Germany. Association for Computational Linguistics.

Karin Kipper Schuler. 2005. *VerbNet: A broad-coverage, comprehensive verb lexicon*. University of Pennsylvania.

Jacob Solawetz and Stefan Larson. 2021. Lsoie: A large-scale dataset for supervised open information extraction. In *EACL*.

Linfeng Song, Daniel Gildea, Yue Zhang, Zhiguo Wang, and Jinsong Su. 2019. Semantic neural machine translation using AMR. *Transactions of the Association for Computational Linguistics*, 7:19–31.

Chuan Wang and Nianwen Xue. 2017. Getting the most out of AMR parsing. In *Proceedings of the 2017 Conference on Empirical Methods in Natural Language Processing*, pages 1257–1268, Copenhagen, Denmark. Association for Computational Linguistics.

Chuan Wang, Nianwen Xue, and Sameer Pradhan. 2015. A transition-based algorithm for AMR parsing. In *Proceedings of the 2015 Conference of the North American Chapter of the Association for Computational Linguistics: Human Language Technologies*, pages 366–375, Denver, Colorado. Association for Computational Linguistics.

Charles Welch, Jonathan K. Kummerfeld, Song Feng, and Rada Mihalcea. 2018. World knowledge for Abstract Meaning Representation parsing. In *Proceedings of the Eleventh International Conference on Language Resources and Evaluation (LREC 2018)*, Miyazaki, Japan. European Language Resources Association (ELRA).

Dongqin Xu, Junhui Li, Muhua Zhu, Min Zhang, and Guodong Zhou. 2020. Improving amr parsing with sequence-to-sequence pre-training. *arXiv preprint arXiv:2010.01771*.

Nianwen Xue and Martha Palmer. 2004. Calibrating features for semantic role labeling. In *EMNLP*, pages 88–94.

Hongming Zhang, Haoyu Wang, and Dan Roth. 2020a. Unsupervised label-aware event trigger and argument classification. *ArXiv*, abs/2012.15243.

Hongming Zhang, Haoyu Wang, and Dan Roth. 2021. Zero-shot label-aware event trigger and argument classification. In *FINDINGS*.

Meishan Zhang, Peilin Liang, and Guohong Fu. 2019a. Enhancing opinion role labeling with semantic-aware word representations from semantic role labeling. In *NAACL*.

Sheng Zhang, Xutai Ma, Kevin Duh, and Benjamin Van Durme. 2019b. AMR parsing as sequence-to-graph transduction. In *Proceedings of the 57th Annual Meeting of the Association for Computational Linguistics*, pages 80–94, Florence, Italy. Association for Computational Linguistics.

Zhuosheng Zhang, Yuwei Wu, Zhao Hai, Z. Li, Shuailiang Zhang, Xi Zhou, and Xiang Zhou. 2020b. Semantics-aware bert for language understanding. *ArXiv*, abs/1909.02209.

Hai Zhao, Wenliang Chen, and Chunyu Kit. 2009. Semantic dependency parsing of NomBank and PropBank: An efficient integrated approach via a large-scale feature selection. In *Proceedings of the 2009 Conference on Empirical Methods in Natural Language Processing*, pages 30–39, Singapore. Association for Computational Linguistics.

Jiawei Zhou, Tahira Naseem, Ramón Fernandez Astudillo, and Radu Florian. 2021. Amr parsing with action-pointer transformer. *arXiv preprint arXiv:2104.14674*.

Qiji Zhou, Yue Zhang, Donghong Ji, and Hao Tang. 2020. AMR parsing with latent structural information. In *Proceedings of the 58th Annual Meeting of the Association for Computational Linguistics*, pages 4306–4319, Online. Association for Computational Linguistics.

Tutorial Abstract

Arabic Natural Language Processing

Nizar Habash
Computational Approaches to Modeling Language (CAMeL) Lab
New York University Abu Dhabi
nizar.habash@nyu.edu

Abstract

The Arabic language continues to be the focus of an increasing number of projects in natural language processing (NLP) and computational linguistics (CL). This tutorial provides NLP/CL system developers and researchers (computer scientists and linguists alike) with the necessary background information for working with Arabic in its various forms: Classical, Modern Standard and Dialectal. We discuss various Arabic linguistic phenomena and review the state-of-the-art in Arabic processing from enabling technologies and resources, to common tasks and applications. The tutorial will explain important concepts, common wisdom, and common pitfalls in Arabic processing. Given the wide range of possible issues, we invite tutorial attendees to bring up interesting challenges and problems they are working on to discuss during the tutorial.

Type of Tutorial: Introductory.

1 Tutorial Description

The purpose of this tutorial is to provide system developers and researchers in natural language processing (NLP) and computational linguistics (CL) with the necessary background information for working with the Arabic language (Modern Standard Arabic, Classical Arabic and Arabic Dialects). The goal is to introduce Arabic linguistic phenomena that need to be addressed from orthography and phonology, to morphology, syntax and semantics, as well as to review the state-of-the-art on Arabic processing from enabling technologies and resources, to common tasks and applications. Alternative approaches will be presented and contrasted for their value in different application contexts. The tutorial will explain important concepts, common wisdom, common pitfalls, as well as basic skills for handling Arabic text, even when illiterate in the Arabic script.

2 Tutorial Outline

This tutorial introduces the different challenges and current solutions to the automatic processing of Arabic and its dialects. The tutorial has three parts (60 minutes each). The second part will be split into two portions, 30 minutes before the coffee break, and 30 minutes after.

Part 1: Arabic NLP Challenges We present the main challenges Arabic poses for NLP. Topics include Arabic script and orthography, orthographic ambiguity and noise, Arabic morphology, morphological richness, complexity and ambiguity, Arabic syntactic and semantic considerations, and Arabic dialectal variations and their challenges.

Part 2: Arabic NLP Solutions We review the state-of-the-art in Arabic NLP covering several enabling technologies and applications, e.g., transliteration schemes, morphological processing (analysis, disambiguation, tokenization, POS tagging), orthographic normalization, dialect identification, text analytics, syntactic parsing, and language modeling. Throughout the presentation we will make references to the different resources and tools available including discussing Arabic annotation standards, tools, and best practices. We will provide links to recent publications and available toolkits and resources.

Part 3: Arabic NLP New Frontiers In this section, we highlight some of the latest efforts and open problems in Arabic NLP, from work on summarization to text simplification, spelling and grammar correction, and gender rewriting. We review the various ongoing Arabic NLP shared tasks and discuss the directions the field is going into, while drawing on historical trends and patterns. This part will interactively draw on the audience and their interests in Arabic NLP.

Proceedings of the 2022 Conference on Empirical Methods in Natural Language Processing: Tutorial Abstracts, pages 9 - 10
December 7-8, 2022

3 Prerequisites

This is an introductory tutorial. No previous knowledge in Arabic is needed. This tutorial is designed for computer scientists and linguists alike. Acquaintance with basic formal language theory and knowledge of some programming languages will be useful.

4 Preparatory Pointers

The following are a set of optional *initial* pointers that will help the attendees maximize their learning experience.

Readings and Lectures

- A panoramic survey of natural language processing in the Arab world [Arxiv version with extended bibliography] (Darwish et al., 2021).
- Arabic Natural Language Processing: Challenges and Solutions [YouTube] (Habash, 2019).
- The Introduction to Arabic Natural Language Processing book (Habash, 2010).

Resources

- Masader+: The Arabic NLP data catalogue: [GitHub] (Alyafeai et al., 2022).
- CAMeL Tools: A suite of Arabic NLP tools [GitHub] (Obeid et al., 2020).
- Farasa: A full-stack package for Arabic Language Processing [Website] (Abdelali et al., 2016).

Sites

- SIGARAB: The ACL Special Interest Group on Arabic Natural Language Processing `http://www.sigarab.org/`, [Mailing List]
- The Arabic Natural Language Processing Workshop (WANLP) [Google Scholar]
- The Workshop on Open-Source Arabic Corpora and Processing Tools (OSACT) [Google Scholar]

Your Ideas and Questions Given the wide range of possible topics, we invite tutorial attendees to come prepared with interesting challenges and problems they are working on to discuss during the tutorial.

5 Tutorial Instructor

Nizar Habash is a Professor of Computer Science at New York University Abu Dhabi (NYUAD). He is also the director of the Computational Approaches to Modeling Language (CAMeL) Lab. Professor Habash specializes in natural language processing and computational linguistics. Before joining NYUAD in 2014, he was a research scientist at Columbia University's Center for Computational Learning Systems. He received his PhD in Computer Science from the University of Maryland College Park in 2003. He has two bachelors degrees, one in Computer Engineering and one in Linguistics and Languages. His research includes extensive work on machine translation, morphological analysis, and computational modeling of Arabic and its dialects. Professor Habash has been a principal investigator or co-investigator on over 25 research grants. And he has over 250 publications including a book entitled "Introduction to Arabic Natural Language Processing" (Habash, 2010). His website is at `www.nizarhabash.com`.

References

Ahmed Abdelali, Kareem Darwish, Nadir Durrani, and Hamdy Mubarak. 2016. Farasa: A Fast and Furious Segmenter for Arabic. In *Proceedings of the North American Chapter of the Association for Computational Linguistics*, San Diego, California.

Zaid Alyafeai, Maraim Masoud, Mustafa Ghaleb, and Maged S. Al-shaibani. 2022. Masader: Metadata sourcing for Arabic text and speech data resources. In *Proceedings of the Language Resources and Evaluation Conference*, Marseille, France.

Kareem Darwish, Nizar Habash, Mourad Abbas, Hend Al-Khalifa, Huseein T Al-Natsheh, Houda Bouamor, Karim Bouzoubaa, Violetta Cavalli-Sforza, Samhaa R El-Beltagy, Wassim El-Hajj, et al. 2021. A panoramic survey of natural language processing in the Arab world. *Communications of the ACM*, 64(4):72–81.

Nizar Habash. 2010. *Introduction to Arabic natural language processing*, volume 3. Morgan & Claypool Publishers.

Nizar Habash. 2019. Arabic natural language processing: Challenges and solutions. Grammarly AI-NLP Club #8, Kyiv, Ukraine.

Ossama Obeid, Nasser Zalmout, Salam Khalifa, Dima Taji, Mai Oudah, Bashar Alhafni, Go Inoue, Fadhl Eryani, Alexander Erdmann, and Nizar Habash. 2020. CAMeL Tools: An open source python toolkit for Arabic natural language processing. In *Proceedings of The Language Resources and Evaluation Conference*, Marseille, France.

Emergent Language-Based Coordination In Deep Multi-Agent Systems

Marco Baroni
Universitat Pompeu Fabra
mbaroni@gmail.com

Roberto Dessì
Universitat Pompeu Fabra
Facebook AI Research
rdessi@fb.com

Angeliki Lazaridou
DeepMind
angeliki@deepmind.com

Abstract

Large pre-trained deep networks are the standard building blocks of modern AI applications. This raises fundamental questions about how to control their behaviour and how to make them efficiently interact with each other. Deep net emergent communication tackles these challenges by studying how to induce communication protocols between neural network agents, and how to include humans in the communication loop. Traditionally, this research had focussed on relatively small-scale experiments where two networks had to develop a discrete code from scratch for referential communication. However, with the rise of large pre-trained language models that can work well on many tasks, the emphasis is now shifting on how to let these models interact through a language-like channel to engage in more complex behaviors. By reviewing several representative papers, we will provide an introduction to deep net emergent communication, we will cover various central topics from the present and recent past, as well as discussing current shortcomings and suggest future directions. The presentation is complemented by a hands-on section where participants will implement and analyze two emergent communications setups from the literature. The tutorial should be of interest to researchers wanting to develop more flexible AI systems, but also to cognitive scientists and linguists interested in the evolution of communication systems.

Brief description and motivation

Just like interaction and communication are pivotal to humans engaging in complex problem solving and coordination, communication among artificial agents allow for effective coordination (both when they cooperate and when they compete). While multi-agent communication protocols can be prespecified and coded, emergent communication has emerged as a successful paradigm – agents are left free to create protocols whose semantics are not pre-determined by any form of supervision, but are rather shaped by the need to achieve their goals.

This utilitarian view of communication is familiar to linguistics (Wittgenstein, 1953). As such, initial work on multi-agent emergent communication studied the conditions under which artificial agents in constrained setups would evolve shared protocols and the latter's similarity to human language (Kirby and Hurford, 1997; Wagner et al., 2003; Steels, 1997). Recently, and after a break of some years, the topic of emergent communication has re-emerged, partially due to the successful and widespread use of deep learning in many fields. In addition to using these simulations to understand the underpinnings of natural language, much work in the field today focuses on how deep network agents could evolve robust protocols, on whether these protocols are interpretable and how it is possible to make them more natural-language-like, in order to enable human-machine communication. Given this recent turn, we started seeing papers on this topic appearing at the major NLP conferences and occasionally being recognized with best-paper awards (Kottur et al., 2017). We believe this is the right time to bring together researchers that wish to know more about the field by offering a structured tutorial on the theme.

Given the interdisciplinarity of the topic, a computational linguistics conference would allow us to reach researchers interested in it from diverse perspectives: AI and NLP researchers who want to develop flexible and robust agents able to coordinate in natural language, but also cognitive scientists/linguists wishing to use simulations to test theories about language evolution.

We will start with an introduction to the emerging field of emergent communication. We will discuss foundational work and we will introduce common experimental setups (i.e., data, training algorithms, analysis and protocol interpretability

Proceedings of the 2022 Conference on Empirical Methods in Natural Language Processing: Tutorial Abstracts, pages 11 - 16
December 7-8, 2022

methods). We will also critically examine the standard practices in the field. Having established the basics, we will then move to discussing promising current directions (i.e., beyond simplistic simulations, linking emergent language to natural language and emerging protocols in situated environments). We will conclude with a hands-on session to deepen attendees' understanding of core concepts by grounding them in actual experiments, but also providing an entry point for researchers who wish to learn how to design such simulations.

Tutorial Structure

The tutorial is divided into 3 slots of around half hour, 1 and a half hour, and 1 hour, respectively. We will have 15 minutes break between each section.

Introduction Early work investigated the necessary conditions for emergence of a shared communication code among artificial agents. Experiments often employed hand-crafted models and/or very simplified environments, and the simulations focused on studying linguistic properties of the emergent protocols (Batali, 1998; Cangelosi and Parisi, 2002; Christiansen and Kirby, 2003).

Recent progress in deep (reinforcement) learning and its successful application in several fields has revamped interest in language emergence. Unlike earlier work, the use of powerful general-purpose neural network models enables experiments with agents that can interact and communicate in complex and dynamic environments. This has led to the introduction of new setups probing language-based coordination between deep agents (Sukhbaatar et al., 2016; Foerster et al., 2016; Mordatch and Abbeel, 2018). Examples of collaborative tasks in "deep emergent communication" include developing a shared code to solve riddles, crossing intersections or goal-oriented navigation.

Another line of research in deep emergent communication focuses on one of the most basic functions of human communication, namely that of referring to a specific object in the surrounding environment. The ability to denote specific items is the building block for more complex forms of collaboration, such as object use and manipulation. Work in this area tends to use a discrimination task called *referential game* (Lewis, 1969). In the game, a sender Agent generates a message that describes a target object. The message is transmitted to a Receiver agent that is tasked with recognizing the object of interest from a set of candidates. Initial work in this domain showed that agents evolve an effective communication policy to denote the content of realistic images (Lazaridou et al., 2017; Havrylov and Titov, 2017). However, later experimental findings suggested that the agents' "language" does not point to semantically meaningful concepts, relying instead on low-level visual features. Subsequent work showed that, unless explicitly constrained, emergent protocols do not develop core properties similar to natural languages, such as compositionality and efficient coding (Chaabouni et al., 2019; Rita et al., 2020). This highlights the importance of bridging the gap between emergent and natural languages, a topic that we will return to in the second part of the tutorial.

Communication between agents in typical setups happens through the exchange of either continuous or discrete messages. In this tutorial, we will focus on experiments with a discrete channel, a prerequisite for language-like human-machine communication. Channel discretization poses an important optimization challenge, given that it is not possible to back-propagate gradients through discrete nodes. We will cover the main approach to overcome this problem that is based on a widely policy gradients method, namely a varient of the REINFORCE algorithm (Williams, 1992).

Given the lack of supervision on the emergent protocol, it is not sufficient to evaluate agents' accuracy on the target task. Such performance-based analysis must be complemented by an analysis of the evolved protocol. This is a far-from-trivial task, somewhat akin to linguistic fieldwork. We will thus end the first part of the tutorial reviewing standard quantitative and qualitative protocol analysis methods currently used in the literature. (Brighton and Kirby, 2006; Lazaridou et al., 2018; Chaabouni et al., 2020; Lowe et al., 2019)

Current themes in emergent communication In the second part, we will introduce in more detail three currently "hot" topics in emergent communication research, presenting main findings along with possible research directions.

The first theme is whether deep nets can communicate about their visual input on a large scale. Lazaridou et al. (2017) showed that two interacting agents can develop a shared lexicon to describe natural images from standard computer vision datasets. The setup of Lazaridou and colleagues used single-symbols messages and sampled images from a limited set of image categories.

Later work by Havrylov and Titov (2017) and Dessi et al. (2021) scaled the visual referential game to variable-length messages and a richer pool of object categories, respectively. Another line of research tries to study the biases that emergent protocols have and whether they are similar to natural language features (Chaabouni et al., 2019, 2020). An example is the work of Rita et al. (2020), it studies which optimization constraints can lead to the emergence of languages that exhibit a human-like word-length distribution. We are still far, however, from robust and flexible visually-aware interactive agents. For instance, most simulations employ a single pair of agents in single-turn interactions, and there is currently no evidence that the emergent protocol will support successful communication with new partners. Additionally, contextual information is not modeled by the agents' protocol, whereas there is ample evidence that human language relies on contextual knowledge to discriminate objects (Glaser and Glaser, 1989; Munneke et al., 2013).

A second important theme is the ability to collaborate in more realistic, dynamic scenarios. Starting from the fully cooperative symbolic agents of Foerster et al. (2016), follow-up work looked at how to integrate different aspects of realistic coordination as they unfold between human agents. For instance, Evtimova et al. (2018) studied multi-turn interactions in a multimodal discrimination task. Das et al. (2019) experimented with embodied agents cooperating to solve a target-reaching navigation task in naturalistic 3D environments. Finally, all these experimental configurations are tied to a single task. On the other hand, natural language allows coordination to be carried out for an unlimited number of goals. However, scaling the an emergent communication setup does not come free of challenges (Chaabouni et al., 2022; Carroll et al., 2019). Future research directions should also investigate the ability of the emergent lexicon to adapt to new tasks, without forgetting those previously learnt.

The third research line studies how emergent protocols can be constrained to resemble natural language and how such languages can be used to interact with large pre-trained networks. Several approaches attempted to interleave game-playing with supervised tasks such as image labelling (Lazaridou et al., 2017; Gupta et al., 2019) and multimodal grounding (Lee et al., 2019), or tried to optimize the agents' communication based on statistics inferred from natural language corpora (Havrylov and Titov, 2017). However, later evidence found that this type of interlaced learning does not protect against forms of pragmatic drift where emergent and natural language interpretation diverges (Lazaridou et al., 2020). Yao et al. (2022) used emergent protocols as a pre-training corpus for image captioning and language modelling, showing performance benefits on downstream tasks. This shows how these protocols could be applied to improve standard NLP tasks, hinting at some structural similarities between emergent and natural languages. Language prompting have recently shown to be effective to extract information from large pre-trained models that are able to excel at many tasks. Such prompts, often manually designed, can be used to combine several powerful and diverse multimodal models (Zeng et al., 2022). Deng et al. (2022) shows how automatic prompt discovery, a method similar to language emergence in deep agents, can improve over several other prompting methods.

Future work should bridge the gap between the language evolved in interactive simulations, usually consisting of short denotational messages, and the syntactic and semantic knowledge acquired by deep networks pre-trained on static large-scale datasets. Additionally how these emergent languages can be used to interact with large and powerful pre-trained models remains an important open challenge.

Hands-on session The final part of the tutorial consists in an interactive hands-on session using EGG (Kharitonov et al., 2021), a Python toolkit designed to offer an easy entry point into emergent communication simulations. By providing implementations of common neural network architectures and simulation setups, it allows developers to quickly code and run a language emergence experiment on both CPU and GPU devices.

In this interactive coding session, we will guide the audience through two experimental setups. In a first configuration, we experiment with a realistic scenario involving natural data. We will provide pre-trained agents that, through a large-scale visual discrimination task, successfully converged on a shared communication policy. We will then probe the agents' communication skills by analysing the messages triggered by unseen input images. This exercise will give the audience a flavor for common challenges involved in interpreting agents' protocol.

In the second half of the session, we will show

how emergent protocols could be used to interact with (large) language models. We will show how automatic discovery of prompts can be used to extract information from pre-trained task-agnostic networks for downstream NLP tasks. This will show the connection between emergent communication and modern NLP.

Further information

Presenters **Marco Baroni** is ICREA research professor at Universitat Pompeu Fabra. **Angeliki Lazaridou** is staff research scientist at DeepMind. Marco and Angeliki co-authored one of the earliest and most influential papers on emergent communication among deep net agents (Lazaridou et al., 2017) as well as a recent survey of the area (Lazaridou and Baroni, 2020). Marco has extensive teaching experience, including interdisciplinary classes aimed at computer scientists, linguists and cognitive scientists, and lectures and tutorials in international venues such as ESSLLI, ACL and the CIFAR Deep Learning Summer School (where he presented an introduction to deep net emergent communication). He was recently awarded an ERC Advanced Grant to work on emergent communication. Angeliki's work in the area was recognized with a 2019 ICML best-paper mention (Jaques et al., 2019). She co-initiated the Emergent Communication Neurips Workshop series (which ran successfully for 6 years). **Roberto Dessì** is a 3rd-year PhD student at Facebook AI Research and Universitat Pompeu Fabra. His work focuses on scaling up emergent communication research, including a paper on the topic to appear at NeurIPS 2021. Roberto was a co-organizer of the last two Emergent Communication workshops and is currently the maintainer of the EGG toolkit for emergent communication simulations.

Tutorial type and breadth We propose a tutorial on an emerging area that has not been previously covered in ACL/EMNLP/NAACL/COLING tutorials. While we are active researchers in the field and we will review some of our own work, the tutorial attempts to survey the area as a whole, as shown by the fact that the majority of references in this proposal are to papers we did not author.

Audience: target, background and size We target two audience types: AI/NLP researchers who might look at emergent communication protocols as a tool to build more flexible multi-agent AI systems; and linguists/cognitive scientists interested in how emergent communication simulations might provide insights into the origins and nature of human and animal communication. The only strict prerequisite consists in basic programming skills in Python, in order to follow the hands-on part of the tutorial. We do not expect the audience to have a technical background in linguistics. While we will rely on standard notions from machine learning, such as cost functions and backpropagation, attendees can get a good high-level view of the area even without this background. This is the first time the tutorial has been offered, but several regular talks by Lazaridou and Baroni introducing the area have registered high attendance. On the one hand, the tutorial has broad interdisciplinary appeal and introduces a novel area to NLP.

Recommended reading While not strictly necessary, participants would benefit from a look at the survey of Lazaridou and Baroni (2020).

Diversity We are a diverse team of instructors, gender-wise and seniority-wise (one senior professor, one senior researcher, one advanced-stage PhD student). We are affiliated with one university and two different industry labs. We expect that the tutorial topic will attract a diverse audience, as it is of interest to both AI/NLP practitioners and linguists/cognitive scientists. While the focus is not on natural language *per se*, we observe that emergent communication research looks at typological research on language variety for inspiration, and it is not reliant on language-specific resources.

Ethics Autonomous agent communication raises ethical issues specifically in terms of *transparency* (see, e.g., `https://ec.europa.eu/digital-single-market/en/high-level-expert-group-artificial-intelligence`). Problems related to the development of opaque protocols (including bias control) and how to spur the emergence of interpretable inter-agent communication will be discussed in the tutorial.

Materials and technical requirements We will use slides and provide scripts for the hands-on part section, where we will use Google Colab and the EGG library (Kharitonov et al., 2021). Attendees should bring a laptop and all materials will be made publicly available.

References

John Batali. 1998. Computational simulations of the emergence of grammar. In James Hurford, Michael Studdert-Kennedy, and Chris Knight, editors, Approaches to the Evolution of Language: Social and Cognitive Bases, pages 405–426. Cambridge University Press, Cambridge, UK.

Henry Brighton and Simon Kirby. 2006. Understanding linguistic evolution by visualizing the emergence of topographic mappings. Artificial Life, 12:229–242.

Angelo Cangelosi and Domenico Parisi. 2002. Computer simulation: A new scientific approach to the study of language evolution. In Simulating the evolution of language, pages 3–28. Springer.

Micah Carroll, Rohin Shah, Mark K Ho, Tom Griffiths, Sanjit Seshia, Pieter Abbeel, and Anca Dragan. 2019. On the utility of learning about humans for human-ai coordination. In Advances in Neural Information Processing Systems, volume 32. Curran Associates, Inc.

Rahma Chaabouni, Eugene Kharitonov, Diane Bouchacourt, Emmanuel Dupoux, and Marco Baroni. 2020. Compositionality and generalization in emergent languages. In Proceedings of ACL, pages 4427–4442, virtual conference.

Rahma Chaabouni, Eugene Kharitonov, Emmanuel Dupoux, and Marco Baroni. 2019. Anti-efficient encoding in emergent communication. In Proceedings of NeurIPS, Vancouver, Canada. Published online: `https://papers.nips.cc/paper/2019`.

Rahma Chaabouni, Florian Strub, Florent Altché, Eugene Tarassov, Corentin Tallec, Elnaz Davoodi, Kory Wallace Mathewson, Olivier Tieleman, Angeliki Lazaridou, and Bilal Piot. 2022. Emergent communication at scale. In International Conference on Learning Representations.

Morten Christiansen and Simon Kirby, editors. 2003. Language Evolution. Oxford University Press, Oxford, UK.

Abhishek Das, Théophile Gervet, Joshua Romoff, Dhruv Batra, Devi Parikh, Mike Rabbat, and Joelle Pineau. 2019. Tarmac: Targeted multi-agent communication. In International Conference on Machine Learning, pages 1538–1546. PMLR.

Mingkai Deng, Jianyu Wang, Cheng-Ping Hsieh, Yihan Wang, Han Guo, Tianmin Shu, Meng Song, Eric P. Xing, and Zhiting Hu. 2022. Rlprompt: Optimizing discrete text prompts with reinforcement learning.

Roberto Dessi, Eugene Kharitonov, and Marco Baroni. 2021. Interpretable agent communication from scratch (with a generic visual processor emerging on the side). In Advances in Neural Information Processing Systems.

Katrina Evtimova, Andrew Drozdov, Douwe Kiela, and Kyunghyun Cho. 2018. Emergent communication in a multi-modal, multi-step referential game. In Proceedings of ICLR Conference Track, Vancouver, Canada. Published online: `https://openreview.net/group?id=ICLR.cc/2018/Conference`.

Jakob Foerster, Ioannis Alexandros Assael, Nando de Freitas, and Shimon Whiteson. 2016. Learning to communicate with deep multi-agent reinforcement learning. In Proceedings of NIPS, pages 2137–2145, Barcelona, Spain.

Wilhelm R Glaser and Margrit O Glaser. 1989. Context effects in stroop-like word and picture processing. Journal of Experimental Psychology: General, 118(1):13.

Abhinav Gupta, Ryan Lowe, Jakob Foerster, Douwe Kiela, and Joelle Pineau. 2019. Seeded self-play for language learning. In Proceedings of the Beyond Vision and LANguage: inTEgrating Real-world kNowledge (LANTERN), pages 62–66, Hong Kong, China. Association for Computational Linguistics.

Serhii Havrylov and Ivan Titov. 2017. Emergence of language with multi-agent games: Learning to communicate with sequences of symbols. In Proceedings of NIPS, pages 2149–2159, Long Beach, CA.

Natasha Jaques, Angeliki Lazaridou, Edward Hughes, Caglar Gulcehre, Pedro Ortega, Dj Strouse, Joel Leibo, and Nando De Freitas. 2019. Social influence as intrinsic motivation for multi-agent deep reinforcement learning. In Proceedings of ICML, pages 3040–3049, Long Beach, CA.

Eugene Kharitonov, Roberto Dessì, Rahma Chaabouni, Diane Bouchacourt, and Marco Baroni. 2021. EGG: a toolkit for research on Emergence of lanGuage in Games. `https://github.com/facebookresearch/EGG`.

Simon Kirby and James Hurford. 1997. Learning, culture and evolution in the origin of linguistic constraints. In Fourth European conference on artificial life, pages 493–502. Citeseer.

Satwik Kottur, José Moura, Stefan Lee, and Dhruv Batra. 2017. Natural language does not emerge 'naturally' in multi-agent dialog. In Proceedings of EMNLP, pages 2962–2967, Copenhagen, Denmark.

Angeliki Lazaridou and Marco Baroni. 2020. Emergent multi-agent communication in the deep learning era. `https://arxiv.org/abs/2006.02419`.

Angeliki Lazaridou, Karl Moritz Hermann, Karl Tuyls, and Stephen Clark. 2018. Emergence of linguistic communication from referential games with symbolic and pixel input. In Proceedings of ICLR Conference Track, Vancouver, Canada. Published online: `https://openreview.net/group?id=ICLR.cc/2018/Conference`.

Angeliki Lazaridou, Alexander Peysakhovich, and Marco Baroni. 2017. Multi-agent cooperation and the emergence of (natural) language. In Proceedings of ICLR Conference Track, Toulon, France. Published online: https://openreview.net/group?id=ICLR.cc/2017/conference.

Angeliki Lazaridou, Anna Potapenko, and Olivier Tieleman. 2020. Multi-agent communication meets natural language: Synergies between functional and structural language learning. In Proceedings of the 58th Annual Meeting of the Association for Computational Linguistics, pages 7663–7674, Online. Association for Computational Linguistics.

Jason Lee, Kyunghyun Cho, and Douwe Kiela. 2019. Countering language drift via visual grounding. In Proceedings of the 2019 Conference on Empirical Methods in Natural Language Processing and the 9th International Joint Conference on Natural Language Processing (EMNLP-IJCNLP), pages 4385–4395, Hong Kong, China. Association for Computational Linguistics.

David Lewis. 1969. Convention. Harvard University Press, Cambridge, MA.

Ryan Lowe, Jakob Foerster, Y-Lan Boureau, Joelle Pineau, and Yann Dauphin. 2019. On the pitfalls of measuring emergent communication. In Proceedings of AAMAS, pages 693–701, Montreal, Canada.

Igor Mordatch and Pieter Abbeel. 2018. Emergence of grounded compositional language in multi-agent populations. In Proceedings of AAAI, pages 1495–1502, New Orleans, LA.

Jaap Munneke, Valentina Brentari, and Marius Peelen. 2013. The influence of scene context on object recognition is independent of attentional focus. Frontiers in Psychology, 4:552.

Mathieu Rita, Rahma Chaabouni, and Emmanuel Dupoux. 2020. "LazImpa": Lazy and impatient neural agents learn to communicate efficiently. In Proceedings of the 24th Conference on Computational Natural Language Learning, pages 335–343, Online. Association for Computational Linguistics.

Luc Steels. 1997. The synthetic modeling of language origins. Evolution of communication, 1(1):1–34.

Sainbayar Sukhbaatar, arthur szlam, and Rob Fergus. 2016. Learning multiagent communication with backpropagation. In Advances in Neural Information Processing Systems, volume 29. Curran Associates, Inc.

Kyle Wagner, James A Reggia, Juan Uriagereka, and Gerald S Wilkinson. 2003. Progress in the simulation of emergent communication and language. Adaptive Behavior, 11(1):37–69.

Ronald Williams. 1992. Simple statistical gradient-following algorithms for connectionist reinforcement learning. Machine learning, 8(3-4):229–256.

Ludwig Wittgenstein. 1953. Philosophical investigations. Blackwell, Oxford, UK.

Shunyu Yao, Mo Yu, Yang Zhang, Karthik R Narasimhan, Joshua B. Tenenbaum, and Chuang Gan. 2022. Linking emergent and natural languages via corpus transfer.

Andy Zeng, Maria Attarian, Brian Ichter, Krzysztof Choromanski, Adrian Wong, Stefan Welker, Federico Tombari, Aveek Purohit, Michael Ryoo, Vikas Sindhwani, Johnny Lee, Vincent Vanhoucke, and Pete Florence. 2022. Socratic models: Composing zero-shot multimodal reasoning with language. arXiv.

CausalNLP Tutorial: An Introduction to Causality for Natural Language Processing

Zhijing Jin
Max Planck Institute & ETH Zürich
jinzhi@ethz.ch

Amir Feder
Columbia University & Google Research
amir.feder@columbia.edu

Kun Zhang
Carnegie Mellon University & MBZUAI
kunz1@cmu.edu

Abstract

Causal inference is becoming an increasingly important topic in deep learning, with the potential to help with critical deep learning problems such as model robustness, interpretability, and fairness. In addition, causality is naturally widely used in various disciplines of science, to discover causal relationships among variables and estimate causal effects of interest. In this tutorial, we introduce the fundamentals of causal discovery and causal effect estimation to the natural language processing (NLP) audience, provide an overview of causal perspectives to NLP problems, and aim to inspire novel approaches to NLP further. This tutorial is inclusive to a variety of audiences and is expected to facilitate the community's developments in formulating and addressing new, important NLP problems in light of emerging causal principles and methodologies.

1 Introduction

Establishing causal relationships is a fundamental goal of scientific research (Pearl, 2000; Spirtes et al., 2001). It naturally boils down to questions of causality when we need to quantify the effectiveness of a vaccine, the persuasive power of a public health ad, or the impact of a lockdown policy: How would the treatment (e.g., vaccine) affect the outcome (e.g., infection rates) compared to a counterfactual world with no treatment? Once formally identified, the direction and strength of causal relationships play a key role in the formulation of clinical treatments, public policy, and other long-standing prescriptive strategies. With such broad applications, a growing body of literature focuses on the interplay between NLP and causal inference (Tan et al., 2014; Wood-Doughty et al., 2018; Sridhar and Getoor, 2019; Veitch et al., 2020; Keith et al., 2020; Feder et al., 2021c).

Despite the interdisciplinary interest in causal inference with text, research in this space seems to remain scattered across domains without clear definitions, notations, benchmark datasets, and an understanding of the state of the art and challenges that remain. For example, it is unclear how deficiencies in NLP methods (such as their inaccuracy with low-resource languages and their tendency to propagate biases in the data) affect downstream causal estimates. In addition, hyperparameter selection and modeling assumptions in NLP are motivated by accuracy and tractability considerations; how these choices affect downstream causal estimates is underexplored.

This tutorial aims to address three questions: (1) What is causality? (2) How can the causal formulation help improve NLP models? (3) How can causality help NLP and computational social science to discover causal phenomena in our society?

Specifically, we will first introduce the fundamentals of causality for the NLP audience, then review research using the causal formulation to help NLP models (in terms of robustness, fairness, and interpretability), and finally introduce how causality can help NLP and computational social science to discover causal relations behind social phenomena.

2 Tutorial Overview

This introductory tutorial aims to introduce causality to the NLP research community. While causality plays a major role in scientific research, it has only now started to disseminate into the NLP community. This is why this tutorial will first focus on providing a generalized introduction to causality and its importance and relevance to the NLP community. We will then dive into the intersection of causality and NLP, and divide it into two distinct areas: using causal formalisms to make NLP methods more interpretable, robust and fair, and discovering causal relations in social phenomena that involve text variables. Accordingly, we divide the content of the tutorial into the following three parts:

Proceedings of the 2022 Conference on Empirical Methods in Natural Language Processing: Tutorial Abstracts, pages 17 - 22
December 7-8, 2022

1. Introduction to Causality. We will give a broad coverage of central concepts, principles, and technical developments in causal modeling; identification of causal effects (known as causal effect estimation); and finding causal relations by analyzing observational data (known as causal discovery). We will focus on representations and usage of causal models (Pearl, 2000; Spirtes et al., 2001), how causality is different from and connected to association, and recent machine learning methods for causal discovery and causal representation learning (Spirtes et al., 2001; Peters et al., 2017; Spirtes and Zhang, 2016; Shimizu et al., 2006; Zhang and Hyvärinen, 2009; Xie et al., 2020, 2022; Huang et al., 2022; Yao et al., 2022).

Specifically, we will answer the following questions: How can we define causality? Is causality an indispensable notion in science and machine learning? Why do we care about causality? How can we infer the causal effect of one variable on another? How can one learn causality from purely observational data? How can we recover latent causal variables and their relations?

2. Causality to Help Improve NLP Models. In this part of the tutorial, we will first motivate the audience by introducing why and how the causal perspective helps in a class of machine learning or AI tasks (Schölkopf et al., 2021; Pearl and Bareinboim, 2011; Schölkopf et al., 2012; Zhang et al., 2013, 2020). Briefly, although deep learning models achieve impressive performance by using correlations for prediction tasks, there are still limitations in their robustness, interpretability and fairness, which could be improved using causality.

With these motivations, we will then extend the causal formulation to NLP. Here, we will identify and highlight existing limitations in NLP methods, and will propose three application areas where causal ideas might help: interpretability (Guidotti et al., 2018), robustness (e.g., McCoy et al., 2019) and fairness (e.g., Zhao et al., 2017). For each potential application area, we will highlight the relevance of causal thinking in solving important open problems in NLP (Feder et al., 2021c; Veitch et al., 2021; Kilbertus et al., 2017).

3. Causality for NLP and Computational Social Science. Distinct from how causality can help improve NLP models in Part 2, we can also see another important use of NLP: identifying causal relations for NLP and computational social science. For example, does there exist gender bias in the upvotes of online posts (Veitch et al., 2020)? Do social media opinions affect the strictness of the COVID-19 social distancing policies (Jin et al., 2021b)? What are the reasons behind popular tweets? Many of these social problems involve text data. For example, online posts, news articles, scientific papers, conversation records, and many others are all text variables. If we want to investigate causal questions, such as the effect of certain contents or features of text on a certain outcome, then we need to run statistical causal models with text modeling.

In this part, we will first introduce how to conduct text-involved causal effect estimation discovery and causal discovery. Then, we will cover some real-world examples where we can apply these methods (Veitch et al., 2020; Feder et al., 2021b; Jin et al., 2021b; Ding et al., 2022; Keidar et al., 2022), and finally run through some exercise questions.

3 Tutorial Outline

For the three-hour tutorial, we will use 2.5 hours to cover three main topics: introduction of causality, how causality can help improve NLP models, and how causality can be applied to NLP and computational social science. And finally, we will use the remaining 30 minutes for an interactive exercise and Q&A.

An outline of the tutorial content is as follows:

1. Introduction to causality (60-min lecture + 5-min break)
   - Motivations: What is causality? Why is causality helpful for NLP?
   - Main content: Basics of causal effect estimation, causal discovery, and causal representation learning.
   - Example work: Pearl (2000); Feder et al. (2021b); Xie et al. (2020); Yao et al. (2022).
2. Causality to help improve NLP models (60-min lecture + 5-min break)
   - Motivations: If the goal is to help improve NLP models, how can causality help? What are some use case examples?
   - Main content: Inspirations from causality to help a variety of NLP topics: model robustness, domain adaptation, debiasing models, interpretability, and fairness.
   - Example work: Schölkopf et al. (2021); Feder et al. (2021c); Veitch et al. (2021);

Jin et al. (2021c); Stolfo et al. (2022); Hupkes et al. (2022).

3. Applications of causality for NLP and computational social science (20-min lecture)
   - Motivations: If the goal is to identify causal phenomena in our society, how can we learn causality on variables that involve text?
   - Main content: Use of SCMs and potential outcomes for NLP social applications such as explaining social media behavior, political phenomena, effective education, and gender bias in the research community. We will also cover cases where causal discovery and inference can help verify linguistic theories.
   - Example work: Veitch et al. (2020); Jin et al. (2021b); Ding et al. (2022).
4. Interactive exercise (20 min)
   - Given a social application of NLP, we will let the audience draw the causal graph, and brainstorm interesting research questions.
   - Given a fairness question in NLP, we will let the audience draw the causal graph, and discuss the causal formulation.
5. Q&A (10 min)

4 Tutorial Breadth

As for the contents of this tutorial, we will mainly cover beginner-friendly introductory materials of NLP, from the studies of established causality researchers out of the NLP domain, such as Judea Pearl, Donald Rubin, Bernhard Schölkopf, Clark Glymour, and Peter Spirtes. Apart from the work from these causality researchers, when it comes to the more specific connection of NLP and causality, we will cover the research work of various researchers: Dyanya Sridhar (Mila), Victor Veitch (University of Chicago), Zach Wood-Doughty (Northwestern University), Justin Grimmer (Stanford), Brandon M. Stewart (Princeton), Margaret E. Roberts (UCSD), Reid Pryzant (Microsoft), and many others.

5 Organizing Committee

Zhijing Jin (she/her) is a PhD at Max Planck Institute and ETH Zürich supervised by Prof Bernhard Schölkopf. Her research aims to (1) improve NLP models by connecting NLP with causal inference (Jin et al., 2021c,b; Ni et al., 2022), and (2) expand the impact of NLP by promoting NLP for social good (Jin et al., 2021a; Field et al., 2021; Gonzalez et al., 2022). She has published at many NLP and AI venues (e.g., AAAI, ACL, EMNLP, NAACL, COLING, AISTATS), and NLP for healthcare venues (e.g., AAHPM, JPSM). To foster the causality research community, she serves as the Publications Chair for the 1st conference on Causal Learning and Reasoning (CLeaR) (Schölkopf et al., 2022). She is also actively involved in AI for social good, as the organizer of NLP for Positive Impact Workshop at ACL 2021 (Field et al., 2021) and EMNLP 2022, and RobustML workshop at ICLR 2021. To support the NLP research community, she organizes the ACL Year-Round Mentorship program from 2021.

Amir Feder (he/him) is a postdoc at Columbia University, working with Prof David Blei. Amir develops methods that integrate causality into natural language processing to generate more robust and interpretable models. He is also interested in investigating and developing linguistically informed algorithms for predicting and understanding human behavior. Amir is currently also a visiting researcher (part time) at Google Research's Medical Brain Team, where he works on methods that leverage causal methodology for medical language models. He is a co-organizer of the First Workshop on Causal Inference and NLP (CI+NLP) at EMNLP 2021 (Feder et al., 2021a).

Kun Zhang (he/him) is an associate professor at Carnegie Mellon University and MBZUAI. His research interests lie in causal discovery and causality-based learning. He develops methods for automated causal discovery from various kinds of data, investigates learning problems including transfer learning and deep learning from a causal view, and studies philosophical foundations of causation and machine learning. He co-authored a best student paper for the Conference on Uncertainty in Artificial Intelligence (UAI) and a best finalist paper for the Conference on Computer Vision and Pattern Recognition (CVPR), and received the best benchmark award of the 2nd causality challenge. He has taken essential roles at many events of causal inference, including the general and program co-chair of the 1st Conference on Causal Learning and Reasoning (CLeaR 2022), program co-chair of the UAI 2022, co-organizer of the 9th Causal Inference Workshop at UAI 2021, co-organizer of NeurIPS 2020 Workshop on Causal Discovery and Causality-Inspired Machine Learning, 2020, co-editor of a number of journal special issues on causality, and many others.

6 Diversity Efforts

Our organizing committee includes both junior and senior instructors, as well as diverse genders, racial/ethnic backgrounds, and affiliations across America, Europe and Asia, which will help make people from various backgrounds feel more welcome to our workshop.

The topic of our workshop is causal inference, which can serve as a helpful tool for many NLP tasks, and the methods can scale up to various languages and domains. In addition, we advertise the tutorial to diversity-oriented venues (e.g., Widening NLP, QueerInAI, BlackInAI, WiML).

7 Target Audience & Prerequisites

There is no required audience background. Preferred knowledge includes the basics of statistics (e.g., understanding of probability distribution of single variables, joint probability distributions, and conditional probability distributions), and the basics of NLP (e.g., understanding of sentence embeddings, and the setup of simple NLP tasks such as classification).

8 Recommended Reading List

We compiled a recommended reading list of causality and NLP papers at (Jin, 2021).[1] Among the papers, the top three recommended readings are Guo et al. (2020), Schölkopf et al. (2021) and Feder et al. (2021b).

9 Other Information

Tutorial Type: Introductory.
Tutorial Materials: We will make available on our GitHub (Jin, 2021) all tutorial presentation materials, including slides, captioned video recordings, codes, and the recommended paper list.

10 Ethical Considerations

The theme of the tutorial focuses on introducing the method of causal inference to NLP. The introduction materials will stay on the technical side. There will not be direct links to applications that will raise ethical concerns. Additionally, since one of the instructor's research background is NLP for social good, we will introduce some use cases of NLP and causal inference for social good applications.

[1] `https://github.com/zhijing-jin/Causality4NLP_Papers`

References

Yiwen Ding, Jiarui Liu, Zhiheng Lyu, Kun Zhang, Bernhard Schoelkopf, Zhijing Jin, and Rada Mihalcea. 2022. Voices of her: Analyzing gender differences in the AI publication world.

Amir Feder, Katherine Keith, Emaad Manzoor, Reid Pryzant, Dhanya Sridhar, Zach Wood-Doughty, Jacob Eisenstein, Justin Grimmer, Roi Reichart, Molly Roberts, Uri Shalit, Brandon Stewart, Victor Veitch, and Diyi Yang, editors. 2021a. *Proceedings of the First Workshop on Causal Inference and NLP*. Association for Computational Linguistics, Punta Cana, Dominican Republic.

Amir Feder, Katherine A. Keith, Emaad Manzoor, Reid Pryzant, Dhanya Sridhar, Zach Wood-Doughty, Jacob Eisenstein, Justin Grimmer, Roi Reichart, Margaret E. Roberts, Brandon M. Stewart, Victor Veitch, and Diyi Yang. 2021b. Causal inference in natural language processing: Estimation, prediction, interpretation and beyond. *CoRR*, abs/2109.00725.

Amir Feder, Nadav Oved, Uri Shalit, and Roi Reichart. 2021c. CausaLM: Causal model explanation through counterfactual language models. *Comput. Linguistics*, 47(2):333–386.

Anjalie Field, Shrimai Prabhumoye, Maarten Sap, Zhijing Jin, Jieyu Zhao, and Chris Brockett, editors. 2021. *Proceedings of the 1st Workshop on NLP for Positive Impact*. Association for Computational Linguistics, Online.

Fernando Gonzalez, Zhijing Jin, Jad Beydoun, Bernhard Schölkopf, Tom Hope, Mrinmaya Sachan, and Rada Mihalcea. 2022. How is NLP addressing the UN Sustainable Development Goals? a challenge set to analyze NLP for social good papers.

Riccardo Guidotti, Anna Monreale, Salvatore Ruggieri, Franco Turini, Fosca Giannotti, and Dino Pedreschi. 2018. A survey of methods for explaining black box models. *ACM computing surveys (CSUR)*, 51(5):1–42.

Ruocheng Guo, Lu Cheng, Jundong Li, P. Richard Hahn, and Huan Liu. 2020. A survey of learning causality with data: Problems and methods. *ACM Comput. Surv.*, 53(4):75:1–75:37.

Biwei Huang, Charles Low, Feng Xie, Clark Glymour, and Kun Zhang. 2022. Latent hierarchical causal structure discovery with rank constraints. In *Neural Information Processing Systems (NeurIPS)*.

Dieuwke Hupkes, Mario Giulianelli, Verna Dankers, Mikel Artetxe, Yanai Elazar, Tiago Pimentel, Christos Christodoulopoulos, Karim Lasri, Naomi Saphra, Arabella Sinclair, Dennis Ulmer, Florian

Schottmann, Khuyagbaatar Batsuren, Kaiser Sun, Koustuv Sinha, Leila Khalatbari, Maria Ryskina, Rita Frieske, Ryan Cotterell, and Zhijing Jin. 2022. State-of-the-art generalisation research in NLP: a taxonomy and review. *CoRR*, abs/2210.03050.

Zhijing Jin. 2021. Causality for NLP reading list. `https://github.com/zhijing-jin/Causality4NLP_Papers`.

Zhijing Jin, Geeticka Chauhan, Brian Tse, Mrinmaya Sachan, and Rada Mihalcea. 2021a. How good is NLP? A sober look at NLP tasks through the lens of social impact. In *Findings of the Association for Computational Linguistics: ACL-IJCNLP 2021*, pages 3099–3113, Online. Association for Computational Linguistics.

Zhijing Jin, Zeyu Peng, Tejas Vaidhya, Bernhard Schoelkopf, and Rada Mihalcea. 2021b. Mining the cause of political decision-making from social media: A case study of COVID-19 policies across the US states. In *Findings of the Association for Computational Linguistics: EMNLP 2021*, pages 288–301, Punta Cana, Dominican Republic. Association for Computational Linguistics.

Zhijing Jin, Julius von Kügelgen, Jingwei Ni, Tejas Vaidhya, Ayush Kaushal, Mrinmaya Sachan, and Bernhard Schoelkopf. 2021c. Causal direction of data collection matters: Implications of causal and anticausal learning for NLP. In *Proceedings of the 2021 Conference on Empirical Methods in Natural Language Processing*, pages 9499–9513, Online and Punta Cana, Dominican Republic. Association for Computational Linguistics.

Daphna Keidar, Andreas Opedal, Zhijing Jin, and Mrinmaya Sachan. 2022. Slangvolution: A causal analysis of semantic change and frequency dynamics in slang. In *Proceedings of the 60th Annual Meeting of the Association for Computational Linguistics (Volume 1: Long Papers)*, pages 1422–1442, Dublin, Ireland. Association for Computational Linguistics.

Katherine Keith, David Jensen, and Brendan O'Connor. 2020. Text and causal inference: A review of using text to remove confounding from causal estimates. In *ACL*.

Niki Kilbertus, Mateo Rojas-Carulla, Giambattista Parascandolo, Moritz Hardt, Dominik Janzing, and Bernhard Schölkopf. 2017. Avoiding discrimination through causal reasoning. In *Proceedings of the 31st International Conference on Neural Information Processing Systems*, pages 656–666.

R Thomas McCoy, Ellie Pavlick, and Tal Linzen. 2019. Right for the wrong reasons: Diagnosing syntactic heuristics in natural language inference. *arXiv preprint arXiv:1902.01007*.

Jingwei Ni, Zhijing Jin, Markus Freitag, Mrinmaya Sachan, and Bernhard Schölkopf. 2022. Original or translated? A causal analysis of the impact of translationese on machine translation performance. In *Proceedings of the 2022 Conference of the North American Chapter of the Association for Computational Linguistics: Human Language Technologies*, pages 5303–5320, Seattle, United States. Association for Computational Linguistics.

J. Pearl. 2000. *Causality: Models, Reasoning, and Inference*. Cambridge University Press, Cambridge.

J. Pearl and E. Bareinboim. 2011. Transportability of causal and statistical relations: A formal approach. In *Proc. AAAI 2011*, pages 247–254.

Jonas Peters, Dominik Janzing, and Bernhard Schölkopf. 2017. *Elements of causal inference: foundations and learning algorithms*. The MIT Press.

B. Schölkopf, D. Janzing, J. Peters, E. Sgouritsa, K. Zhang, and J. Mooij. 2012. On causal and anticausal learning. In *ICML-12*, Edinburgh, Scotland.

Bernhard Schölkopf, Francesco Locatello, Stefan Bauer, Nan Rosemary Ke, Nal Kalchbrenner, Anirudh Goyal, and Yoshua Bengio. 2021. Towards causal representation learning. *CoRR*, abs/2102.11107.

Bernhard Schölkopf, Caroline Uhler, and Kun Zhang, editors. 2022. *Proceedings of the First Conference on Causal Learning and Reasoning*, volume 177 of *Proceedings of Machine Learning Research*. PMLR.

S. Shimizu, P.O. Hoyer, A. Hyvärinen, and A.J. Kerminen. 2006. A linear non-Gaussian acyclic model for causal discovery. *Journal of Machine Learning Research*, 7:2003–2030.

P. Spirtes, C. Glymour, and R. Scheines. 2001. *Causation, Prediction, and Search*, 2nd edition. MIT Press, Cambridge, MA.

Peter Spirtes and Kun Zhang. 2016. Causal discovery and inference: concepts and recent methodological advances. In *Applied informatics*, volume 3, pages 1–28. SpringerOpen.

Dhanya Sridhar and Lise Getoor. 2019. Estimating causal effects of tone in online debates. In *International Joint Conference on Artificial Intelligence*.

Alessandro Stolfo, Zhijing Jin, Kumar Shridhar, Bernhard Schoelkopf, and Mrinmaya Sachan. 2022. A causal framework to quantify the model robustness on math word problems.

Chenhao Tan, Lillian Lee, and Bo Pang. 2014. The effect of wording on message propagation: Topic- and author-controlled natural experiments on twitter. In *Proceedings of the 52nd Annual Meeting of the Association for Computational Linguistics (Volume 1: Long Papers)*, pages 175–185.

Victor Veitch, Alexander D'Amour, Steve Yadlowsky, and Jacob Eisenstein. 2021. Counterfactual invariance to spurious correlations: Why and how to pass stress tests. *arXiv preprint arXiv:2106.00545*.

Victor Veitch, Dhanya Sridhar, and David M Blei. 2020. Adapting text embeddings for causal inference. In *UAI*.

Zach Wood-Doughty, Ilya Shpitser, and Mark Dredze. 2018. Challenges of using text classifiers for causal inference. In *EMNLP*.

F. Xie, R. Cai, B. Huang, C. Glymour, Z. Hao, and K. Zhang. 2020. Generalized independent noise condition for estimating linear non-gaussian latent variable causal graphs. In *Neural Information Processing Systems (NeurIPS)*.

Feng Xie, Biwei Huang, Zhengming Chen, Yangbo He, Zhi Geng, and Kun Zhang. 2022. Identification of linear non-Gaussian latent hierarchical structure. In *Proceedings of the 39th International Conference on Machine Learning*, pages 24370–24387.

Weiran Yao, Guangyi Chen, and Kun Zhang. 2022. Causal disentanglement for time series. In *Neural Information Processing Systems (NeurIPS)*.

K. Zhang and A. Hyvärinen. 2009. On the identifiability of the post-nonlinear causal model. In *Proceedings of the 25th Conference on Uncertainty in Artificial Intelligence*, Montreal, Canada.

K. Zhang, B. Schölkopf, K. Muandet, and Z. Wang. 2013. Domain adaptation under target and conditional shift. In *ICML-13*.

Kun Zhang, Mingming Gong, Petar Stojanov, Biwei Huang, Qingsong Liu, and Clark Glymour. 2020. Domain adaptation as a problem of inference on graphical models. In *Neural Information Processing Systems (NeurIPS)*.

Jieyu Zhao, Tianlu Wang, Mark Yatskar, Vicente Ordonez, and Kai-Wei Chang. 2017. Men also like shopping: Reducing gender bias amplification using corpus-level constraints. In *Proceedings of the 2017 Conference on Empirical Methods in Natural Language Processing*, pages 2979–2989, Copenhagen, Denmark. Association for Computational Linguistics.

Modular and Parameter-Efficient Fine-Tuning for NLP Models

Sebastian Ruder
Google Research
ruder@google.com

Jonas Pfeiffer
Google Research
jonaspfeiffer@google.com

Ivan Vulić
LTL, University of Cambridge
iv250@cam.ac.uk

Abstract

State-of-the-art language models in NLP perform best when fine-tuned even on small datasets, but due to their increasing size, fine-tuning and downstream usage have become extremely compute-intensive. Being able to efficiently and effectively fine-tune the largest pre-trained models is thus key in order to reap the benefits of the latest advances in NLP. In this tutorial, we provide a comprehensive overview of parameter-efficient fine-tuning methods. We highlight their similarities and differences by presenting them in a unified view. We explore the benefits and usage scenarios of a neglected property of such parameter-efficient models—modularity—such as composition of modules to deal with previously unseen data conditions. We finally highlight how both properties—parameter efficiency and modularity—can be useful in the real-world setting of adapting pre-trained models to under-represented languages and domains with scarce annotated data for several downstream applications.[1]

1 Motivation and Objectives

The emergence of large pre-trained language models (Devlin et al., 2019) has led to a watershed moment in NLP, accelerating progress and improving performance across a wide range of NLP benchmarks. These models have quickly superseded previous baseline models and are now a core part of every NLP researcher and practitioner's toolkit. While pre-training such models has always been prohibitively expensive, recent pre-trained models have been getting so large (Brown et al., 2020) that even their fine-tuning and downstream usage are extremely challenging. In practice, the largest models perform best, even when fine-tuned on small datasets (Li et al., 2020). Therefore, being able to *efficiently and effectively fine-tune* the largest pre-trained models is key in order to reap the benefits of the latest advances in NLP. This is a major challenge that threatens to further exacerbate the inequality between resource-rich and resource-constrained research and production environments.

Recent work has highlighted the benefit of parameter-efficient methods to fine-tune such large pre-trained models. These parameter-efficient fine-tuning methods include soft prompt methods that preprend a small set of trainable continuous parameters to the input or intermediate layers (Li and Liang, 2021; Lester et al., 2021; Mahabadi et al., 2022), low-rank methods that train a small number of parameters in a low-dimensional subspace using random projections (Li et al., 2018; Aghajanyan et al., 2021), and adapter methods that insert trainable transformations at different layers (Houlsby et al., 2019; Pfeiffer et al., 2020). Other methods only tune a subset of the model's parameters (Lee et al., 2019; Zaken et al., 2021). An alternative set of methods relies on identifying performant sparse subnetworks, which can be updated in isolation (Frankle and Carbin, 2019; Guo et al., 2021; Xu et al., 2021; Sung et al., 2021). These methods reduce not only the number of parameters during fine-tuning but also have been shown to be more robust than standard fine-tuning and to outperform it in low-resource conditions (He et al., 2021b; Han et al., 2021; Mahabadi et al., 2021).

In the *first part* of this tutorial, we will give a comprehensive overview of such parameter-efficient fine-tuning methods. We will highlight the similarities and differences of a wide array of these methods by presenting them in a unified view, which expands on recent work (He et al., 2021a; Mao et al., 2021) highlighting the connections between adapters and prefix tuning. Based on this common view, we will be able to clearly show the respective benefits and trade-offs of a diverse set of parameter-efficient fine-tuning methods.

A commonality of parameter-efficient methods—

[1]Slides are available at: https://tinyurl.com/modular-fine-tuning-tutorial

Proceedings of the 2022 Conference on Empirical Methods in Natural Language Processing: Tutorial Abstracts, pages 23 - 29
December 7-8, 2022 ©2022 Association for Computational Linguistics

illustrated clearly in this framework—is that they learn a modification vector that is added to the pre-trained model parameters, which are kept fixed. This property opens the door to *modularity*, which we view as a neglected benefit of the parameter-efficient usage of pre-trained models.

In the *second part* of the tutorial, we will explore the benefits and usage scenarios of such modular approaches. We will demonstrate how modular 'expert' modules can be learned for specific data settings (Chen et al., 2019; Rücklé et al., 2020; Gururangan et al., 2022; Li et al., 2022). Moreover, they can provide further benefits when combined and adapting to previously unseen settings (Pfeiffer et al., 2021a). We will additionally discuss how modular approaches can be used to augment models with new capabilities or knowledge, such as memory for lifelong learning (Kaiser et al., 2017), numerical reasoning (Andor et al., 2019), and factual or linguistic knowledge (Wang et al., 2021a). A key benefit of modularity is that it enables the storage and composition of modules to deal with previously unseen data conditions (Ponti et al., 2021, 2022). We will highlight this benefit based on prior work (Wortsman et al., 2020; Ponti et al., 2021; Ansell et al., 2022) and explore applications that it may enable in the future. Finally, as an NLP 'history lesson', we will revisit modular approaches that preceded pre-trained models (Andreas et al., 2016) and highlight how they may be relevant for recent approaches. Overall, we will encourage attendees to think of pre-trained models not as monoliths but as building blocks than can be augmented for specific purposes and data settings.

Tying both previous parts together, the *third part* of the tutorial will focus on applications: we will demonstrate how the properties explored so far—parameter efficiency and modularity—can be useful in practical settings. Specifically, we will focus on the important real-world setting of adapting pre-trained models to under-represented languages and domains with scarce annotated data for several downstream applications, e.g., cross-lingual transfer (Pfeiffer et al., 2020, 2022) and NMT (Bapna and Firat, 2019; Philip et al., 2020; Le et al., 2021; Üstün et al., 2021). We will highlight approaches that enable learning language-specific components using previously presented techniques such as adapters (Üstün et al., 2020; Pfeiffer et al., 2020, 2021b; Parović et al., 2022) or sparse subnetworks (Lin et al., 2021; Ansell et al., 2022). We will specifically discuss challenges and possible solutions when using such methods to adapt pre-trained models to extremely low-resource scenarios, such as test time adaptation (Wang et al., 2021b), parameter generation (Platanios et al., 2018; Ansell et al., 2021; Üstün et al., 2022), domain adaptation (Chronopoulou et al., 2022), and usage of alternative data sources (Ebrahimi and Kann, 2021; Faisal and Anastasopoulos, 2022).

1.1 What This Tutorial Does NOT Cover

We focus on parameter-efficient methods for adaptation of pre-trained models and thus only briefly discuss methods to make pre-training itself more efficient via efficient neural network architectures (Tay et al., 2020), including mixture-of-experts layers (Shazeer et al., 2017; Fedus et al., 2021). We will only briefly mention the emerging but already extensive literature on prompting,[2] and discuss its connections to the main topic of this tutorial. While prompting is itself parameter-efficient (requiring zero parameters) and can be combined with the fine-tuning methods we discuss, an extensive discussion of prompting would require its own tutorial. For similar reasons, we will only briefly highlight the extensive literature on controllable text generation. We will also only briefly discuss other techniques to improve efficiency such as knowledge distillation as these have been covered by the recent High Performance Natural Language Processing tutorial at EMNLP 2020 (Ilharco et al., 2020).

1.2 Tutorial Specifications

Tutorial Type: Cutting-edge, 3 hours

Target Audience: The target audience are researchers and practitioners in NLP who are interested in 1) extending research on this topic as well as 2) using state-of-the-art pre-trained models efficiently. In addition, target audience members will become familiar with diverse ways to make use of pre-trained models, beyond the standard prompting or fine-tuning setup.

Prerequisites: The target audience should be familiar with common neural network architectures (e.g., attention, Transformers), and also have a basic understanding of contemporary approaches in NLP, such as standard pre-trained models.

[2]For a comprehensive survey discussing prompting methods, we refer to (Liu et al., 2021).

2 Tutorial Outline

In what follows, we provide finer-grained descriptions of the main topics covered in the tutorial, along with tentative time allocation:

2.1 Parameter-efficient Models *[1h 10 mins]*

1. **Overview of Parameter-efficient Models** *[35 mins]*: We will begin the tutorial by introducing our audience to the range of techniques and methods used to fine-tune NLP models in a parameter-efficient way, from prompt tuning and adapters to pruning-based approaches. We will motivate the necessity and importance of research on parameter efficiency, and the main benefits of these approaches. To highlight a more pragmatic motivation, a comprehensive list of current and potential applications will also be provided.

2. **A Unified View of Parameter Efficiency** *[35 mins]*: We will provide the audience with a unified view of the parameter-efficient methods presented thus far. We will employ this view to highlight the key dimensions along which existing approaches differ as well as detail the resulting trade-offs that different approaches make. As part of this section, we will also provide a systematic general overview of the performance and computational efficiency of representative methods on an array of diverse benchmarks. In general, we will aim to provide the audience with a sense of the 'design space' of parameter-efficient methods so that they will not only be able to employ current methods, but expand and build upon them in future research.

2.2 Coffee Break *[30 mins]*

2.3 Modular Models *[55 minutes]*

1. **Learning Modular Experts** *[25 minutes]*: We will first highlight how modular experts can be learned in different settings and how these experts can be used to adapt to novel data distributions. We will also discuss how experts can provide access to new capabilities or new types of knowledge, such as numerical reasoning or factual and linguistic knowledge.

2. **Storing and Composing Modules** *[15 minutes]*: Having described the general setting and scenarios where modularity can be useful, we will highlight how modularity can lead to extremely efficient storage as well as composition of modules to adapt to unseen data settings: in the long run, the modular design leads to (re)composable and more sustainable NLP methods.

3. **Modularity Before Pre-training** *[15 minutes]*: We will finally revisit classic modular approaches and describe how some of the techniques and lessons from prior work may be applicable to the current generation of models.

2.4 Application: Multilingual and Low-Resource NLP *[55 minutes]*

1. **Parameter-efficient Methods for Multilingual NLP** *[25 minutes]*: In the last part of the tutorial, we will describe how the previosly discussed methods can be used to adapt pre-trained models to low-resource scenarios, with a focus on adapting pre-trained multilingual models to under-represented languages and domains, and enhancing multilingual NMT models for such resource-poor languages. This part focuses mainly on how language-specific components can be learned effectively, and how they can be combined with domain-specific and task-specific components, reaping the benefits of the modular design (from the previous part). This section will also discuss very recent methods based on efficient multilingual and language-specific contextual parameter generation and learning language-specific sub-networks. We will also highlight connections to pre-neural research on parameter-efficient methods for multilingual NLP.

2. **Adapting to Extremely Low-resource Languages** *[15 minutes]*: In addition, we will discuss challenges when learning such modular components in the extremely low-resource settings that are common when dealing with under-represented languages. Going beyond data scarcity, we will highlight challenges when learning languages with a different script, word order, or rich morphology. We will then describe strategies that can be used to effectively adapt models to such languages, including the use of external information (e.g., linguistic typology) to condition and enrich the modular design.

3. **Open Research Directions** *[15 minutes]*: In the last section, we will provide the audience

with an overview of research directions in this area and key pointers that will help them to pursue their own research, and apply the current technology in downstream NLP applications. Some time will also be reserved for a short QA session with the presenters.

3 Diversity

The third part of the tutorial focuses on how the described methods can be applied to improve models especially for low-resource and under-represented languages. This aligns with a long-term aim and promise of multilingual NLP to bring language technology to virtually *any* language of the world. We aim to make scripts available that demonstrate how the discussed methods can be applied in this setting. We hope this will help to diversify the audience, especially in the emerging regions such as Africa and Central and South America, and make the tutorial accessible to both beginners and advanced researchers.

4 Ethics Statement

The methodology introduced in the tutorial potentially inherits standard undesirable biases stemming from pretraining language models on large (and unverified) multilingual text collections. During the tutorial, we will ensure to remind NLP researchers and practitioners to bear in mind these biases, and apply appropriate data filtering and debiasing techniques before deploying any text encoders and relevant methodology to real-world language technology applications.

5 Presenters

Name: Sebastian Ruder
Affiliation: Google Research
Email: `ruder@google.com`
Website: `http://ruder.io`
Sebastian is a research scientist at Google Research where he works on transfer and cross-lingual learning and on parameter-efficient models. He was the Program Co-Chair for EurNLP 2019 and has co-organized the 4th Workshop on Representation Learning for NLP at ACL 2019 and the First Workshop on Multilingual Representation Learning at EMNLP 2021 and 2022. He has taught tutorials on "Transfer learning in natural language processing", "Unsupervised Cross-lingual Representation Learning", and "Multi-domain Multilingual Question Answering" at NAACL 2019, ACL 2019, and EMNLP 2021 respectively. He has also co-organized and taught at the NLP Session at the Deep Learning Indaba 2018, 2019, and 2022.

Name: Jonas Pfeiffer
Affiliation: Google Research
Email: `jonaspfeiffer@google.com`
Website: `https://pfeiffer.ai`
Jonas is a research scientist at Google Research. He is interested in modular and compositional representation learning in multi-task, multilingual, and multi-modal contexts. Jonas has received the IBM PhD Research Fellowship award in 2020. He has given invited talks in academia (e.g. University of Cambridge, ETH, EPFL, NYU), industry (e.g. Facebook AI Research, IBM Research), as well as at Machine Learning Summer/Winter Schools (e.g. Lisbon ML Summer School (LxMLS) 2021, Advanced Language Processing Winter School (ALPS) 2022).

Name: Ivan Vulić
Affiliation: University of Cambridge & PolyAI
Email: `iv250@cam.ac.uk`
Website: `https://sites.google.com/site/ivanvulic/`
Ivan is a Principal Research Associate and a Royal Society University Research Fellow in the Language Technology Lab at the University of Cambridge, and a Senior Scientist at PolyAI. His research interests are in multilingual and multimodal representation learning, and transfer learning for low-resource languages and applications such as task-oriented dialogue systems. He has extensive experience giving invited and keynote talks, and co-organising tutorials (e.g., ECIR 2013, WSDM 2014, EMNLP 2017, NAACL-HLT 2018, ESSLLI 2018, ACL 2019, 2 tutorials at EMNLP 2019, AILC Lectures 2021, ACL 2022) and workshops in areas relevant to the tutorial proposal (e.g., VL'15, SIGTYP 2019-2021, DeeLIO 2020-2022, RepL4NLP 2021, MML 2022, publication chair of ACL 2019, program chair of *SEM 2021, tutorial co-chair of EMNLP 2021).

6 Acknowledgments

Ivan Vulić is supported by a personal Royal Society University Research Fellowship, and his work has also been supported by a Huawei research donation awarded to the Language Technology Lab.

References

Armen Aghajanyan, Luke Zettlemoyer, and Sonal Gupta. 2021. Intrinsic Dimensionality Explains the Effectiveness of Language Model Fine-Tuning. In *Proceedings of ACL 2021*.

Daniel Andor, Luheng He, Kenton Lee, and Emily Pitler. 2019. Giving BERT a calculator: Finding operations and arguments with reading comprehension. In *Proceedings of the EMNLP 2019*.

Jacob Andreas, Marcus Rohrbach, Trevor Darrell, and Dan Klein. 2016. Learning to Compose Neural Networks for Question Answering. In *Proceedings of NAACL 2016*.

Alan Ansell, Edoardo Ponti, Anna Korhonen, and Ivan Vulić. 2022. Composable sparse fine-tuning for cross-lingual transfer. In *Proceedings of ACL 2022*.

Alan Ansell, Edoardo Maria Ponti, Jonas Pfeiffer, Sebastian Ruder, Goran Glavaš, Ivan Vulić, and Anna Korhonen. 2021. MAD-G: Multilingual adapter generation for efficient cross-lingual transfer. In *Findings of EMNLP 2021*.

Ankur Bapna and Orhan Firat. 2019. Simple, scalable adaptation for neural machine translation. In *Proceedings of EMNLP 2019*.

Tom B. Brown, Benjamin Mann, Nick Ryder, Melanie Subbiah, Jared Kaplan, Prafulla Dhariwal, Arvind Neelakantan, Pranav Shyam, Girish Sastry, Amanda Askell, Sandhini Agarwal, Ariel Herbert-Voss, Gretchen Krueger, Tom Henighan, Rewon Child, Aditya Ramesh, Daniel M. Ziegler, Jeffrey Wu, Clemens Winter, Christopher Hesse, Mark Chen, Eric Sigler, Mateusz Litwin, Scott Gray, Benjamin Chess, Jack Clark, Christopher Berner, Sam McCandlish, Alec Radford, Ilya Sutskever, and Dario Amodei. 2020. Language Models are Few-Shot Learners. In *Advances in NeurIPS 2020*.

Vincent S Chen, Sen Wu, Zhenzhen Weng, Alexander Ratner, and Christopher Ré. 2019. Slice-based learning: A programming model for residual learning in critical data slices. *Advances in NeurIPS 2019*.

Alexandra Chronopoulou, Matthew Peters, and Jesse Dodge. 2022. Efficient hierarchical domain adaptation for pretrained language models. In *Proceedings of NAACL-HLT 2022*.

Jacob Devlin, Ming-Wei Chang, Kenton Lee, and Kristina Toutanova. 2019. BERT: Pre-training of Deep Bidirectional Transformers for Language Understanding. In *Proceedings of NAACL 2019*.

Abteen Ebrahimi and Katharina Kann. 2021. How to Adapt Your Pretrained Multilingual Model to 1600 Languages. In *Proceedings of ACL 2021*.

Fahim Faisal and Antonios Anastasopoulos. 2022. Phylogeny-inspired adaptation of multilingual models to new languages. *CoRR*, abs/2205.09634.

William Fedus, Barret Zoph, and Noam Shazeer. 2021. Switch Transformers: Scaling to Trillion Parameter Models with Simple and Efficient Sparsity. *arXiv preprint*.

Jonathan Frankle and Michael Carbin. 2019. The lottery ticket hypothesis: Finding sparse, trainable neural networks. In *Proceedings of ICLR 2019*.

Demi Guo, Alexander M. Rush, and Yoon Kim. 2021. Parameter-efficient transfer learning with diff pruning. In *Proceedings of ACL 2021*.

Suchin Gururangan, Mike Lewis, Ari Holtzman, Noah A. Smith, and Luke Zettlemoyer. 2022. DEMix layers: Disentangling domains for modular language modeling. In *Proceedings of the NAACL 2022*.

Wenjuan Han, Bo Pang, and Yingnian Wu. 2021. Robust Transfer Learning with Pretrained Language Models through Adapters. In *Proceedings of ACL 2021*.

Junxian He, Chunting Zhou, Xuezhe Ma, Taylor Berg-Kirkpatrick, and Graham Neubig. 2021a. Towards a Unified View of Parameter-Efficient Transfer Learning. *arXiv preprint*.

Ruidan He, Linlin Liu, Hai Ye, Qingyu Tan, Bosheng Ding, Liying Cheng, Jiawei Low, Lidong Bing, and Luo Si. 2021b. On the Effectiveness of Adapter-based Tuning for Pretrained Language Model Adaptation. In *Proceedings of ACL 2021*.

Neil Houlsby, Andrei Giurgiu, Stanislaw Jastrzebski, Bruna Morrone, Quentin de Laroussilhe, Andrea Gesmundo, Mona Attariyan, and Sylvain Gelly. 2019. Parameter-Efficient Transfer Learning for NLP. In *Proceedings of ICML 2019*.

Gabriel Ilharco, Cesar Ilharco, Iulia Turc, Tim Dettmers, Felipe Ferreira, and Kenton Lee. 2020. High performance natural language processing. In *Proceedings of EMNLP 2020: Tutorial Abstracts*.

Łukasz Kaiser, Ofir Nachum, Aurko Roy, and Samy Bengio. 2017. Learning to Remember Rare Events. In *Proceedings of ICLR 2017*.

Hang Le, Juan Pino, Changhan Wang, Jiatao Gu, Didier Schwab, and Laurent Besacier. 2021. Lightweight adapter tuning for multilingual speech translation. In *Proceedings of ACL-IJCNLP 2021*.

Jaejun Lee, Raphael Tang, and Jimmy Lin. 2019. What Would Elsa Do? Freezing Layers During Transformer Fine-Tuning. *arXiv preprint*.

Brian Lester, Rami Al-Rfou, and Noah Constant. 2021. The Power of Scale for Parameter-Efficient Prompt Tuning. In *Proceedings of EMNLP 2021*.

Chunyuan Li, Heerad Farkhoor, Rosanne Liu, and Jason Yosinski. 2018. Measuring the Intrinsic Dimension of Objective Landscapes. In *Proceedings of ICLR 2018*.

Margaret Li, Suchin Gururangan, Tim Dettmers, Mike Lewis, Tim Althoff, Noah A. Smith, and Luke Zettlemoyer. 2022. Branch-train-merge: Embarrassingly parallel training of expert language models. *arXiv preprint*.

Xiang Lisa Li and Percy Liang. 2021. Prefix-tuning: Optimizing continuous prompts for generation. In *Proceedings of ACL 2021*.

Zhuohan Li, Eric Wallace, Sheng Shen, Kevin Lin, Kurt Keutzer, Dan Klein, and Joseph E. Gonzalez. 2020. Train large, then compress: Rethinking model size for efficient training and inference of transformers. *arXiv preprint*.

Zehui Lin, Liwei Wu, Mingxuan Wang, and Lei Li. 2021. Learning language specific sub-network for multilingual machine translation. In *Proceedings of ACL 2021*.

Pengfei Liu, Weizhe Yuan, Jinlan Fu, Zhengbao Jiang, Hiroaki Hayashi, and Graham Neubig. 2021. Pre-train, prompt, and predict: A systematic survey of prompting methods in Natural Language Processing. *arXiv preprint*.

Rabeeh Karimi Mahabadi, James Henderson, and Sebastian Ruder. 2021. Compacter: Efficient Low-Rank Hypercomplex Adapter Layers. In *Advances in NeurIPS 2021*.

Rabeeh Karimi Mahabadi, Luke Zettlemoyer, James Henderson, Lambert Mathias, Marzieh Saeidi, Veselin Stoyanov, and Majid Yazdani. 2022. Prompt-free and efficient few-shot learning with language models. In *Proceedings of ACL 2022*.

Yuning Mao, Lambert Mathias, Rui Hou, Amjad Almahairi, Hao Ma, Jiawei Han, Wen-tau Yih, and Madian Khabsa. 2021. UniPELT: A Unified Framework for Parameter-Efficient Language Model Tuning. *arXiv preprint*.

Marinela Parović, Goran Glavaš, Ivan Vulić, and Anna Korhonen. 2022. BAD-X: Bilingual adapters improve zero-shot cross-lingual transfer. In *Proceedings of NAACL-HLT 2022*.

Jonas Pfeiffer, Naman Goyal, Xi Lin, Xian Li, James Cross, Sebastian Riedel, and Mikel Artetxe. 2022. Lifting the curse of multilinguality by pre-training modular transformers. In *Proceedings of the NAACL 2022*.

Jonas Pfeiffer, Aishwarya Kamath, Andreas Rückle, Cho Kyunghyun, and Iryna Gurevych. 2021a. AdapterFusion: Non-destructive task composition for transfer learning. In *Proceedings of EACL 2021*.

Jonas Pfeiffer, Ivan Vulic, Iryna Gurevych, and Sebastian Ruder. 2020. MAD-X: an adapter-based framework for multi-task cross-lingual transfer. In *Proceedings of EMNLP 2020*.

Jonas Pfeiffer, Ivan Vulić, Iryna Gurevych, and Sebastian Ruder. 2021b. UNKs Everywhere: Adapting Multilingual Language Models to New Scripts. In *Proceedings of EMNLP 2021*.

Jerin Philip, Alexandre Berard, Matthias Gallé, and Laurent Besacier. 2020. Monolingual adapters for zero-shot neural machine translation. In *Proceedings of EMNLP 2020*.

Emmanouil Antonios Platanios, Mrinmaya Sachan, Graham Neubig, and Tom Mitchell. 2018. Contextual parameter generation for universal neural machine translation. In *Proceedings of EMNLP 2018*.

Edoardo M. Ponti, Ivan Vulić, Ryan Cotterell, Marinela Parovic, Roi Reichart, and Anna Korhonen. 2021. Parameter Space Factorization for Zero-Shot Learning across Tasks and Languages. *Transactions of the ACL 2021*.

Edoardo Maria Ponti, Alessandro Sordoni, and Siva Reddy. 2022. Combining modular skills in multitask learning. *CoRR*, abs/2202.13914.

Andreas Rücklé, Jonas Pfeiffer, and Iryna Gurevych. 2020. MultiCQA : Zero-Shot Transfer of Self-Supervised Text Matching Models on a Massive Scale. In *Proceedings of EMNLP 2020*.

Noam Shazeer, Azalia Mirhoseini, Krzysztof Maziarz, Andy Davis, Quoc V. Le, Geoffrey E. Hinton, and Jeff Dean. 2017. Outrageously large neural networks: The sparsely-gated mixture-of-experts layer. In *Proceedings of ICLR 2017*.

Yi-Lin Sung, Varun Nair, and Colin Raffel. 2021. Training neural networks with fixed sparse masks. In *Advances in NeurIPS 2021*.

Yi Tay, Mostafa Dehghani, Dara Bahri, and Donald Metzler. 2020. Efficient Transformers: A Survey. *arXiv preprint*.

Ahmet Üstün, Alexandre Berard, Laurent Besacier, and Matthias Gallé. 2021. Multilingual unsupervised neural machine translation with denoising adapters. In *Proceedings of EMNLP 2021*.

Ahmet Üstün, Arianna Bisazza, Gosse Bouma, and Gertjan van Noord. 2020. UDapter: Language adaptation for truly Universal Dependency parsing. In *Proceedings of EMNLP 2020*.

Ahmet Üstün, Arianna Bisazza, Gosse Bouma, Gertjan van Noord, and Sebastian Ruder. 2022. Hyper-X: A unified hypernetwork for multi-task multilingual transfer. *CoRR*, abs/2205.12148.

Ruize Wang, Duyu Tang, Nan Duan, Zhongyu Wei, Xuanjing Huang, Jianshu Ji, Guihong Cao, Daxin Jiang, and Ming Zhou. 2021a. K-Adapter: Infusing Knowledge into Pre-Trained Models with Adapters. In *Findings of ACL 2021*.

Xinyi Wang, Yulia Tsvetkov, Sebastian Ruder, and Graham Neubig. 2021b. Efficient Test Time Adapter Ensembling for Low-resource Language Varieties. In *Findings of EMNLP 2021*.

Mitchell Wortsman, Vivek Ramanujan, Rosanne Liu, Aniruddha Kembhavi, Mohammad Rastegari, Jason Yosinski, and Ali Farhadi. 2020. Supermasks in Superposition. In *Advances in NeurIPS 2020*.

Runxin Xu, Fuli Luo, Zhiyuan Zhang, Chuanqi Tan, Baobao Chang, Songfang Huang, and Fei Huang. 2021. Raise a Child in Large Language Model : Towards Effective and Generalizable Fine-tuning. In *Proceedings of EMNLP 2021*.

Elad Ben Zaken, Shauli Ravfogel, and Yoav Goldberg. 2021. BitFit: Simple Parameter-efficient Fine-tuning for Transformer-based Masked Language-models. *arXiv preprint*.

Non-Autoregressive Models for Fast Sequence Generation

Yang Feng[1,2] **Chenze Shao**[1,2]
[1] Key Laboratory of Intelligent Information Processing
Institute of Computing Technology, Chinese Academy of Sciences (ICT/CAS)
[2] University of Chinese Academy of Sciences, Beijing, China
{fengyang,shaochenze18z}@ict.ac.cn

1 Tutorial Introduction

Autoregressive (AR) models have achieved great success in various sequence generation tasks (Bahdanau et al., 2015; Vaswani et al., 2017). However, AR models can only generate the target sequence word-by-word due to the AR mechanism and hence suffer from slow inference. Recently, non-autoregressive (NAR) models, which generate all the tokens in parallel by removing the sequential dependencies within the target sequence, have received increasing attention in sequence generation tasks such as neural machine translation (NMT, Gu et al., 2018), automatic speech recognition (ASR, Salazar et al., 2019), and text to speech (TTS, Ren et al., 2019).

Recently, non-autoregressive (NAR) models have received much attention in various sequence generation tasks, which generate all tokens in parallel by ignoring the sequential dependency within the target sequence. Gu et al. (2018) proposed the first NAR translation model for the efficient inference of neural machine translation, and NAR generation has subsequently been applied to a wide range of sequence generation tasks, where the two most successful application scenarios are ASR and TTS. The major challenge faced by NAR generation is the multi-modality problem: there may exist multiple correct outputs for the same source input, but the naive NAR model is unable to capture the multi-modal data distribution. Therefore, the direct application of NAR generation will usually lead to significant performance degradation compared to the autoregressive counterpart.

In this tutorial, we will provide a comprehensive introduction to non-autoregressive sequence generation. First, we start with the background of sequence generation, giving the motivation of NAR generation and the challenge faced by NAR models. We will briefly introduce the autoregressive generation mechanism and autoregressive sequence models that evolve from recurrent neural networks (Schuster and Paliwal, 1997) to self-attention networks (Vaswani et al., 2017). We point out their problems caused by the autoregressive mechanism, including exposure bias (Ranzato et al., 2016), error propagation, fixed generation direction, causal attention, and most importantly, the high inference latency. We will then introduce the NAR model that solves the above-mentioned problems by generating all target tokens in parallel, and point out the multi-modality challenge faced by NAR models (Gu et al., 2018).

Second, we will introduce research work that aims to improve the performance of NAR generation, mainly focusing on non-autoregressive translation in this part. The involved work covers efforts over knowledge distillation (Kim and Rush, 2016; Zhou et al., 2020; Sun and Yang, 2020; Ding et al., 2021; Shao et al., 2022b), better training objectives (Shao et al., 2019, 2020; Ghazvininejad et al., 2020; Du et al., 2021, 2022; Tu et al., 2020; Shao et al., 2021; Shao and Feng, 2022; Li et al., 2022b; Anonymous, 2023), latent modeling (Gu et al., 2018; Kaiser et al., 2018; Ma et al., 2019; Ran et al., 2021; Song et al., 2021; Shu et al., 2020; Bao et al., 2021, 2022), more expressive NAR models (Wang et al., 2017; Libovický and Helcl, 2018; Sun et al., 2019; Huang et al., 2022), improved decoding approaches (Lee et al., 2018; Ghazvininejad et al., 2019; Gu et al., 2019; Ran et al., 2020; Saharia et al., 2020; Deng and Rush, 2020; Geng et al., 2021; Stern et al., 2018, 2019; Xia et al., 2022; Shao et al., 2022a), etc.

Third, we will introduce NAR models on other sequence generation tasks, where the two most successful application scenarios are ASR and TTS. The idea of NAR generation was first pervading in ASR, where Graves et al. (2006) proposed the CTC network which predicts outputs independently, but the recurrent network architecture prevents it from parallel decoding. With the emergence of paralleliz-

Proceedings of the 2022 Conference on Empirical Methods in Natural Language Processing: Tutorial Abstracts, pages 30 - 35
December 7-8, 2022

able self-attention network (Vaswani et al., 2017), CTC-based NAR models soon became a promising direction in ASR (Higuchi et al., 2020; Chen et al., 2020). In TTS, parallel generation is particularly necessary due to the extremely large length of output sequence. The first attempt is Parallel WaveNet (Oord et al., 2018) which keeps the autoregressive mechanism but enables parallel generation with inverse autoregressive flow (Kingma et al., 2016). NAR models are subsequently proposed for TTS (Ren et al., 2019, 2020a; Prenger et al., 2019), which caught up with AR models in a short time and soon became the mainstream method for TTS.

We will also introduce other applications of NAR models like language modeling (Huang et al., 2021; Li et al., 2022a), image/video captioning (Gao et al., 2019; Yang et al., 2021), dialogue generation (Wu et al., 2020; Le et al., 2020), and even object detection (Carion et al., 2020). It is observed that NAR models perform well on some tasks but suffer from performance degradation on other tasks. This phenomenon can be explained from the perspective of multi-modality (Gu et al., 2018) or target token dependency (Ren et al., 2020b).

Finally, we will conclude this tutorial by summarizing the strengths and challenges of NAR models and discussing current concerns and future directions of NAR generation.

2 Type of Tutorial

The type of tutorial is cutting-edge. Non-autoregressive generation is a newly emerging topic, which has attracted increasing attention from researchers and achieved remarkable advancement in the past several years. This is the second tutorial on this topic in the history of ACL, EMNLP, NAACL, EACL, COLING, and AACL (Gu and Tan, 2022).

3 Tutorial Outline

Part I: Introduction (20 min)

- Autoregressive sequence generation
- Problems of AR generation
  - High inference latency
  - Exposure bias
  - Error propagation
- Non-autoregressive generation
- Multi-modality challenge

Part II: Non-Autoregressive Machine Translation (80 min)

- Knowledge distillation
- Training objectives
  - Token-level
  - Ngram-level
  - Sequence-level
- Latent modeling
  - Variational autoencoder
  - Vector quantization
  - Word alignment
- Expressive NAR models
  - CTC
  - DA-Transformer
- Decoding approaches
  - Iterative decoding
  - Semi-autoregressive decoding
  - Speculative decoding

Part III: Non-Autoregressive Sequence Generation (60 min)

- Non-autoregressive ASR
- Non-autoregressive TTS
- Other generation tasks
  - language modeling
  - Image/video captioning
  - Dialogue generation
  - Object detection
- What kind of tasks are NAR models good at?
  - Multi-modality
  - Target token dependency

Part IV: Conclusion (20 min)

4 Breadth

This tutorial will provide a comprehensive introduction to non-autoregressive sequence generation. We anticipate that at least 90% of the tutorial will cover work by other researchers.

5 Diversity

In the past, NAR sequence generation usually involves one or two languages. Recently, some researchers have found that NAR models are good at multilingual translation (Song et al., 2022), which may stimulate the progress of NAR generation in multilingual scenarios.

Yang Feng is a senior instructor and Chenze Shao is a junior instructor.

6 Prerequisites

The attendees have to understand the basics of neural networks and the sequence-to-sequence framework, including word embeddings, encoder-decoder models, and the Transformer architecture.

7 Reading List

We recommend attendees to read the following papers before the tutorial:

- Vaswani et al. (2017): the parallelizable Transformer network based on attention mechanisms.
- Gu et al. (2018): first propose non-autoregressive generation for parallel decoding and point out the multi-modality problem.
- Kim and Rush (2016): train the student model with the teacher output, alleviating the multi-modality by reducing data complexity.
- Shao et al. (2021): train NAR models with sequence-level objectives, which evaluate model outputs as a whole and optimize the overall translation quality.
- Shu et al. (2020): use latent variables to model the non-determinism in the translation process.
- Ghazvininejad et al. (2019): iteratively refine model outputs by repeatedly masking out and regenerating partial target tokens.
- Graves et al. (2006): the early exploration of non-autoregressive generation, and the proposed CTC loss is widely used in recent NAR models.
- Ren et al. (2019): non-autoregressive text-to-speech model, which matches autoregressive models in terms of speech quality.
- Ren et al. (2020b): a study on NAR models that analyzes the difficulty of NAR generation on different generation tasks

8 Tutorial Presenters

Yang Feng is a professor in Institute of Computing Technology, Chinese Academy of Sciences (ICT/CAS). She got her PhD degree in ICT/CAS and then worked in University of Sheffield and Information Sciences Institute, University of Southern California, and now leads the natural language processing group in ICT/CAS. Her research interests are natural language process, mainly focusing on machine translation and dialogue. She was the recipient of the Best Long Paper Award of ACL 2019. She served as a senior area chair of EMNLP 2021 and area chairs of ACL, EMNLP, COLING etc., and she is serving as an Action Editor of ACL Roling Review and an editorial board member of the Northern European Journal of Language Technology. She has given a tutorial in the 10th CCF International Conference on Natural Language Processing and Chinese Computing (NLPCC2021) and has been invited to give talks in NLPCC, CCL(China National Conference on Computational Linguistics) etc.

Chenze Shao is a fifth-year PhD student in Institute of Computing Technology, Chinese Academy of Sciences. His research interests are natural language processing and neural machine translation. His recent research topic is non-autoregressive (NAR) sequence generation. He has published papers on NAR generation in CL, ACL, EMNLP, NAACL, AAAI and NeurIPS.

9 Other Information

Technical Requirements This tutorial does not have special requirements for technical equipment.

Ethics Statement The technique of non-autoregressive generation improves the efficiency of text generation and may reduce the cost of generating malicious text.

Open Access. All of our tutorial materials can be shared in the ACL Anthology.

References

Anonymous. 2023. Fuzzy alignments in directed acyclic graph for non-autoregressive machine translation. In *Submitted to The Eleventh International Conference on Learning Representations*. Under review.

Dzmitry Bahdanau, Kyunghyun Cho, and Yoshua Bengio. 2015. Neural machine translation by jointly learning to align and translate. In *3rd International Conference on Learning Representations, ICLR 2015, San Diego, CA, USA, May 7-9, 2015, Conference Track Proceedings*.

Yu Bao, Shujian Huang, Tong Xiao, Dongqi Wang, Xinyu Dai, and Jiajun Chen. 2021. Non-autoregressive translation by learning target categorical codes. In *Proceedings of the 2021 Conference of the North American Chapter of the Association for Computational Linguistics: Human Language Technologies*, pages 5749–5759, Online. Association for Computational Linguistics.

Yu Bao, Hao Zhou, Shujian Huang, Dongqi Wang, Lihua Qian, Xinyu Dai, Jiajun Chen, and Lei Li. 2022. latent-GLAT: Glancing at latent variables for parallel text generation. In *Proceedings of the 60th Annual Meeting of the Association for Computational Linguistics (Volume 1: Long Papers)*, pages 8398–8409, Dublin, Ireland. Association for Computational Linguistics.

Nicolas Carion, Francisco Massa, Gabriel Synnaeve, Nicolas Usunier, Alexander Kirillov, and Sergey Zagoruyko. 2020. End-to-end object detection with transformers. In *European Conference on Computer Vision*, pages 213–229. Springer.

Nanxin Chen, Shinji Watanabe, Jesús Villalba, Piotr Żelasko, and Najim Dehak. 2020. Non-autoregressive transformer for speech recognition. *IEEE Signal Processing Letters*, 28:121–125.

Yuntian Deng and Alexander Rush. 2020. Cascaded text generation with markov transformers. In *Advances in Neural Information Processing Systems*, volume 33, pages 170–181. Curran Associates, Inc.

Liang Ding, Longyue Wang, Xuebo Liu, Derek F. Wong, Dacheng Tao, and Zhaopeng Tu. 2021. Understanding and improving lexical choice in non-autoregressive translation. In *International Conference on Learning Representations*.

Cunxiao Du, Zhaopeng Tu, and Jing Jiang. 2021. Order-agnostic cross entropy for non-autoregressive machine translation. In *Proceedings of the 38th International Conference on Machine Learning, ICML 2021, 18-24 July 2021, Virtual Event*, volume 139 of *Proceedings of Machine Learning Research*, pages 2849–2859. PMLR.

Cunxiao Du, Zhaopeng Tu, Longyue Wang, and Jing Jiang. 2022. ngram-oaxe: Phrase-based order-agnostic cross entropy for non-autoregressive machine translation. *arXiv preprint arXiv:2210.03999*.

Junlong Gao, Xi Meng, Shiqi Wang, Xia Li, Shanshe Wang, Siwei Ma, and Wen Gao. 2019. Masked non-autoregressive image captioning. *arXiv preprint arXiv:1906.00717*.

Xinwei Geng, Xiaocheng Feng, and Bing Qin. 2021. Learning to rewrite for non-autoregressive neural machine translation. In *Proceedings of the 2021 Conference on Empirical Methods in Natural Language Processing*, pages 3297–3308, Online and Punta Cana, Dominican Republic. Association for Computational Linguistics.

Marjan Ghazvininejad, Vladimir Karpukhin, Luke Zettlemoyer, and Omer Levy. 2020. Aligned cross entropy for non-autoregressive machine translation. In *Proceedings of the 37th International Conference on Machine Learning, ICML 2020, 13-18 July 2020, Virtual Event*, volume 119 of *Proceedings of Machine Learning Research*, pages 3515–3523. PMLR.

Marjan Ghazvininejad, Omer Levy, Yinhan Liu, and Luke Zettlemoyer. 2019. Mask-predict: Parallel decoding of conditional masked language models. In *Proceedings of the 2019 Conference on Empirical Methods in Natural Language Processing and the 9th International Joint Conference on Natural Language Processing (EMNLP-IJCNLP)*, pages 6112–6121.

Alex Graves, Santiago Fernández, Faustino Gomez, and Jürgen Schmidhuber. 2006. Connectionist temporal classification: Labelling unsegmented sequence data with recurrent neural networks. In *Proceedings of the 23rd International Conference on Machine Learning*, ICML '06, page 369–376, New York, NY, USA. Association for Computing Machinery.

Jiatao Gu, James Bradbury, Caiming Xiong, Victor O. K. Li, and Richard Socher. 2018. Non-autoregressive neural machine translation. In *6th International Conference on Learning Representations, ICLR 2018, Vancouver, BC, Canada, April 30 - May 3, 2018, Conference Track Proceedings*.

Jiatao Gu and Xu Tan. 2022. Non-autoregressive sequence generation. In *Proceedings of the 60th Annual Meeting of the Association for Computational Linguistics: Tutorial Abstracts*, pages 21–27.

Jiatao Gu, Changhan Wang, and Junbo Zhao. 2019. Levenshtein transformer. In *Advances in Neural Information Processing Systems 32: Annual Conference on Neural Information Processing Systems 2019, NeurIPS 2019, December 8-14, 2019, Vancouver, BC, Canada*, pages 11179–11189.

Yosuke Higuchi, Shinji Watanabe, Nanxin Chen, Tetsuji Ogawa, and Tetsunori Kobayashi. 2020. Mask ctc: Non-autoregressive end-to-end asr with ctc and mask predict. *Proc. Interspeech 2020*, pages 3655–3659.

Fei Huang, Jian Guan, Pei Ke, Qihan Guo, Xiaoyan Zhu, and Minlie Huang. 2021. A text {gan} for language generation with non-autoregressive generator.

Fei Huang, Hao Zhou, Yang Liu, Hang Li, and Minlie Huang. 2022. Directed acyclic transformer for non-autoregressive machine translation. In *Proceedings of the 39th International Conference on Machine Learning, ICML 2022*.

Lukasz Kaiser, Samy Bengio, Aurko Roy, Ashish Vaswani, Niki Parmar, Jakob Uszkoreit, and Noam Shazeer. 2018. Fast decoding in sequence models using discrete latent variables. In *Proceedings of the*

35th International Conference on Machine Learning, volume 80 of *Proceedings of Machine Learning Research*, pages 2390–2399. PMLR.

Yoon Kim and Alexander M. Rush. 2016. Sequence-level knowledge distillation. In *Proceedings of the 2016 Conference on Empirical Methods in Natural Language Processing*, pages 1317–1327, Austin, Texas. Association for Computational Linguistics.

Durk P Kingma, Tim Salimans, Rafal Jozefowicz, Xi Chen, Ilya Sutskever, and Max Welling. 2016. Improved variational inference with inverse autoregressive flow. *Advances in neural information processing systems*, 29:4743–4751.

Hung Le, Richard Socher, and Steven C.H. Hoi. 2020. Non-autoregressive dialog state tracking. In *International Conference on Learning Representations*.

Jason Lee, Elman Mansimov, and Kyunghyun Cho. 2018. Deterministic non-autoregressive neural sequence modeling by iterative refinement. In *Proceedings of the 2018 Conference on Empirical Methods in Natural Language Processing*, pages 1173–1182, Brussels, Belgium. Association for Computational Linguistics.

Xiang Lisa Li, John Thickstun, Ishaan Gulrajani, Percy Liang, and Tatsunori B Hashimoto. 2022a. Diffusion-lm improves controllable text generation. *arXiv preprint arXiv:2205.14217*.

Yafu Li, Leyang Cui, Yongjing Yin, and Yue Zhang. 2022b. Multi-granularity optimization for non-autoregressive translation. In *EMNLP 2022*.

Jindřich Libovický and Jindřich Helcl. 2018. End-to-end non-autoregressive neural machine translation with connectionist temporal classification. In *Proceedings of the 2018 Conference on Empirical Methods in Natural Language Processing*, pages 3016–3021, Brussels, Belgium. Association for Computational Linguistics.

Xuezhe Ma, Chunting Zhou, Xian Li, Graham Neubig, and Eduard Hovy. 2019. FlowSeq: Non-autoregressive conditional sequence generation with generative flow. In *Proceedings of the 2019 Conference on Empirical Methods in Natural Language Processing and the 9th International Joint Conference on Natural Language Processing (EMNLP-IJCNLP)*, pages 4282–4292, Hong Kong, China. Association for Computational Linguistics.

Aaron Oord, Yazhe Li, Igor Babuschkin, Karen Simonyan, Oriol Vinyals, Koray Kavukcuoglu, George Driessche, Edward Lockhart, Luis Cobo, Florian Stimberg, et al. 2018. Parallel wavenet: Fast high-fidelity speech synthesis. In *International conference on machine learning*, pages 3918–3926. PMLR.

Ryan Prenger, Rafael Valle, and Bryan Catanzaro. 2019. Waveglow: A flow-based generative network for speech synthesis. In *ICASSP 2019-2019 IEEE International Conference on Acoustics, Speech and Signal Processing (ICASSP)*, pages 3617–3621. IEEE.

Qiu Ran, Yankai Lin, Peng Li, and Jie Zhou. 2020. Learning to recover from multi-modality errors for non-autoregressive neural machine translation. In *Proceedings of the 58th Annual Meeting of the Association for Computational Linguistics*, pages 3059–3069, Online. Association for Computational Linguistics.

Qiu Ran, Yankai Lin, Peng Li, and Jie Zhou. 2021. Guiding non-autoregressive neural machine translation decoding with reordering information. In *Thirty-Fifth AAAI Conference on Artificial Intelligence, AAAI 2021, Virtual Event, February 2-9, 2021*, pages 13727–13735. AAAI Press.

Marc'Aurelio Ranzato, Sumit Chopra, Michael Auli, and Wojciech Zaremba. 2016. Sequence level training with recurrent neural networks. In *4th International Conference on Learning Representations, ICLR 2016, San Juan, Puerto Rico, May 2-4, 2016, Conference Track Proceedings*.

Yi Ren, Chenxu Hu, Xu Tan, Tao Qin, Sheng Zhao, Zhou Zhao, and Tie-Yan Liu. 2020a. Fastspeech 2: Fast and high-quality end-to-end text to speech. In *International Conference on Learning Representations*.

Yi Ren, Jinglin Liu, Xu Tan, Zhou Zhao, Sheng Zhao, and Tie-Yan Liu. 2020b. A study of non-autoregressive model for sequence generation. In *Proceedings of the 58th Annual Meeting of the Association for Computational Linguistics*, pages 149–159.

Yi Ren, Yangjun Ruan, Xu Tan, Tao Qin, Sheng Zhao, Zhou Zhao, and Tie-Yan Liu. 2019. Fastspeech: Fast, robust and controllable text to speech. In *Advances in Neural Information Processing Systems 32: Annual Conference on Neural Information Processing Systems 2019, NeurIPS 2019, December 8-14, 2019, Vancouver, BC, Canada*, pages 3165–3174.

Chitwan Saharia, William Chan, Saurabh Saxena, and Mohammad Norouzi. 2020. Non-autoregressive machine translation with latent alignments. In *Proceedings of the 2020 Conference on Empirical Methods in Natural Language Processing (EMNLP)*, pages 1098–1108, Online. Association for Computational Linguistics.

Julian Salazar, Katrin Kirchhoff, and Zhiheng Huang. 2019. Self-attention networks for connectionist temporal classification in speech recognition. *ICASSP 2019 - 2019 IEEE International Conference on Acoustics, Speech and Signal Processing (ICASSP)*.

M. Schuster and K.K. Paliwal. 1997. Bidirectional recurrent neural networks. *IEEE Transactions on Signal Processing*, 45(11):2673–2681.

Chenze Shao and Yang Feng. 2022. Non-monotonic latent alignments for ctc-based non-autoregressive machine translation. In *Proceedings of NeurIPS 2022*.

Chenze Shao, Yang Feng, Jinchao Zhang, Fandong Meng, Xilin Chen, and Jie Zhou. 2019. Retrieving sequential information for non-autoregressive neural machine translation. In *Proceedings of the 57th Annual Meeting of the Association for Computational Linguistics*, pages 3013–3024, Florence, Italy. Association for Computational Linguistics.

Chenze Shao, Yang Feng, Jinchao Zhang, Fandong Meng, and Jie Zhou. 2021. Sequence-Level Training for Non-Autoregressive Neural Machine Translation. *Computational Linguistics*, pages 1–35.

Chenze Shao, Zhengrui Ma, and Yang Feng. 2022a. Viterbi decoding of directed acyclic transformer for non-autoregressive machine translation. In *Findings of EMNLP 2022*.

Chenze Shao, Xuanfu Wu, and Yang Feng. 2022b. One reference is not enough: Diverse distillation with reference selection for non-autoregressive translation. In *Proceedings of the 2022 Conference of the North American Chapter of the Association for Computational Linguistics: Human Language Technologies*, pages 3779–3791, Seattle, United States. Association for Computational Linguistics.

Chenze Shao, Jinchao Zhang, Yang Feng, Fandong Meng, and Jie Zhou. 2020. Minimizing the bag-of-ngrams difference for non-autoregressive neural machine translation. In *The Thirty-Fourth AAAI Conference on Artificial Intelligence, AAAI 2020, New York, NY, USA, February 7-12, 2020*, pages 198–205. AAAI Press.

Raphael Shu, Jason Lee, Hideki Nakayama, and Kyunghyun Cho. 2020. Latent-variable non-autoregressive neural machine translation with deterministic inference using a delta posterior. In *The Thirty-Fourth AAAI Conference on Artificial Intelligence, AAAI 2020, New York, NY, USA, February 7-12, 2020*, pages 8846–8853. AAAI Press.

Jongyoon Song, Sungwon Kim, and Sungroh Yoon. 2021. AligNART: Non-autoregressive neural machine translation by jointly learning to estimate alignment and translate. In *Proceedings of the 2021 Conference on Empirical Methods in Natural Language Processing*, pages 1–14, Online and Punta Cana, Dominican Republic. Association for Computational Linguistics.

Zhenqiao Song, Hao Zhou, Lihua Qian, Jingjing Xu, Shanbo Cheng, Mingxuan Wang, and Lei Li. 2022. switch-GLAT: Multilingual parallel machine translation via code-switch decoder. In *International Conference on Learning Representations*.

Mitchell Stern, William Chan, Jamie Kiros, and Jakob Uszkoreit. 2019. Insertion transformer: Flexible sequence generation via insertion operations. In *Proceedings of the 36th International Conference on Machine Learning*, volume 97 of *Proceedings of Machine Learning Research*, pages 5976–5985. PMLR.

Mitchell Stern, Noam Shazeer, and Jakob Uszkoreit. 2018. Blockwise parallel decoding for deep autoregressive models. *Advances in Neural Information Processing Systems*, 31.

Zhiqing Sun, Zhuohan Li, Haoqing Wang, Di He, Zi Lin, and Zhihong Deng. 2019. Fast structured decoding for sequence models. In *Advances in Neural Information Processing Systems 32*, pages 3016–3026.

Zhiqing Sun and Yiming Yang. 2020. An EM approach to non-autoregressive conditional sequence generation. In *Proceedings of the 37th International Conference on Machine Learning*, volume 119 of *Proceedings of Machine Learning Research*, pages 9249–9258. PMLR.

Lifu Tu, Richard Yuanzhe Pang, Sam Wiseman, and Kevin Gimpel. 2020. ENGINE: Energy-based inference networks for non-autoregressive machine translation. In *Proceedings of the 58th Annual Meeting of the Association for Computational Linguistics*, pages 2819–2826, Online. Association for Computational Linguistics.

Ashish Vaswani, Noam Shazeer, Niki Parmar, Jakob Uszkoreit, Llion Jones, Aidan N. Gomez, undefinedukasz Kaiser, and Illia Polosukhin. 2017. Attention is all you need. In *Proceedings of the 31st International Conference on Neural Information Processing Systems*, NIPS'17, pages 6000–6010, Red Hook, NY, USA. Curran Associates Inc.

Chong Wang, Yining Wang, Po-Sen Huang, Abdelrahman Mohamed, Dengyong Zhou, and Li Deng. 2017. Sequence modeling via segmentations. In *International Conference on Machine Learning*, pages 3674–3683. PMLR.

Di Wu, Liang Ding, Fan Lu, and Jian Xie. 2020. SlotRefine: A fast non-autoregressive model for joint intent detection and slot filling. In *Proceedings of the 2020 Conference on Empirical Methods in Natural Language Processing (EMNLP)*, pages 1932–1937, Online. Association for Computational Linguistics.

Heming Xia, Tao Ge, Furu Wei, and Zhifang Sui. 2022. Lossless speedup of autoregressive translation with generalized aggressive decoding. *arXiv preprint arXiv:2203.16487*.

Bang Yang, Yuexian Zou, Fenglin Liu, and Can Zhang. 2021. Non-autoregressive coarse-to-fine video captioning. In *Proceedings of the AAAI Conference on Artificial Intelligence*, volume 35, pages 3119–3127.

Chunting Zhou, Jiatao Gu, and Graham Neubig. 2020. Understanding knowledge distillation in non-autoregressive machine translation. In *8th International Conference on Learning Representations, ICLR 2020, Addis Ababa, Ethiopia, April 26-30, 2020*.

Author Index